PROVERBS

for

Promise

Keeping

DAYBREAK
PUBLISHERS

P.O. Box 261129 • San Diego, CA 92196

PROVERBS FOR PROMISE KEEPING
© 1996 Daybreak Publishers. All rights reserved.

Unless otherwise noted, Scripture quotations are from the HOLY BIBLE, NEW
INTERNATIONAL VERSION. Copyright © 1973, 1978, 1984 International Bible
Society. Used by permission of Zondervan Bible Publishers.
Scripture marked KJV is taken from the KING JAMES VERSION of the Bible.

No part of this publication may be reproduced, stored in a retrieval system, or
transmitted in any form or by any means–electronic, mechanical, photocopy,
recording, or otherwise–without prior permission of the copyright owner.

Editor: Ron Durham

Cover Design: Stray Cat Studio
               San Diego, CA

Published by Daybreak Publishers
P.O. Box 261129 • San Diego, CA 92196

Printed in the United States of America

Foreword by Gene Getz

The Promise Keepers movement is one of the most encouraging scenes in our times. In our own church, we have seen interest grow from a vanload of guys to several city buses filled with men who have attended these events. What a thrill to see a new sense of motivation and commitment to being men of God.

One concern, however, that always seems to lurk in the shadows is the staying power of the commitments that are made in an emotionally-charged environment. Although I'm not questioning that the decisions made during these rallies are real and sincere, permanent life changes only take place when we are feeding daily on the Word of God. This is why I am excited about Bob's book. All of us have gone to the doctor's office and have made decisions to improve our physical health. However, if anything is going to happen we have to pay daily attention to our physical bodies – proper food and proper exercise. So Paul reminds us to train ourselves to be godly. Although he acknowledges that "physical training has some value," he makes it very clear "that godliness has value for all things" (1 Timothy 4:7, 8). From a spiritual perspective, Bob's book will help us to achieve that goal. It's just "what the doctor ordered."

Proverbs for Promise Keeping provides the "ongoing workout" that all of us need to sustain the seven wonderful promises many men are making. Bob's experience in the army, in business, in the family, and in the church enables him to speak to men right where they are. Furthermore, he has spent time in the Word gleaning the wisdom of Proverbs that will help us to face today's tough issues.

Bob is also an innovator and pioneer, which is reflected in this book. He presents a broad range of biblical models – both positive and negative – which flesh out the timeless proverbial principles. His "one page exhortations" will help you to work them in to your busy schedule on a daily basis.

One proverb we use in our Men's Ministry here at Fellowship Bible Church North is that "as iron sharpens iron so one man sharpens his friend" (Prov. 27:17). I am confident that as you read through these Proverbs, think through the questions Bob has given us, and sincerely pray that God will change your life, you will be sharpened and shaped into the man God wants you to be.

Your friend,

Gene Getz, Ph.D.
Senior Pastor, Fellowship Bible Church North
Director, Center for Church Renewal
Adjunct Professor, Dallas Theological Seminary

Proverbs for Promise Keeping

ABOUT THE AUTHOR

Bob Beasley was born in Nashville, Tennessee, in 1938 but has spent the majority of his life in San Diego, California. Graduated from Claremont McKenna College in 1959, he was discharged a captain in the Army Ordnance Corps in 1963 and began his career in the real estate industry. He served Coldwell, Banker and Company (now CB Commercial) in their mortgage loan and commercial sales divisions before beginning his own development business in 1972. Bob developed residential properties in California, Texas, and Florida. In 1981, he formed Commercial Property Information Services, Inc. (now COMPS InfoSystems), a firm that publishes confirmed market data of commercial property sales throughout the major metropolitan areas of the United States. He is still involved in that company's growth.

Bob was called to Christ in August 1971. Since then he has been involved in teaching adult studies in his church, in speaking at retreats and conferences, and in teaching a number of businessmen's Bible studies, one of which is in its 16th year. He is currently a candidate for a master's degree in theological studies at Westminster Theological Seminary. Bob is married and has three grown daughters. He and his wife, Amy, live in San Diego, where they are members of New Life Orthodox Presbyterian Church.

Proverbs for Promise Keeping is a topical study of the book of Proverbs designed around the general outline provided by *Seven Promises of a Promise Keeper* (Focus on the Family: Colorado Springs, 1994). Its selection of verses is drawn from Bob's completed manuscript, *Proverbs for Everyone,* a devotional/study guide involving the entire book of Proverbs, and soon to be published by Daybreak Publishers.

For Amy...

"He who finds a wife
finds what is good
and receives favor from the Lord."
Proverbs 18:22

...in the Name of the Holy One of Israel.

"The Lord is exalted, for he dwells on high;
he will fill Zion with justice and righteousness.
He will be the sure foundation for your times,
a rich store of salvation and wisdom and knowledge;
the fear of the Lord is the key to this treasure."
Isaiah 33:5, 6

Contents

· ·

Preface

··

If you are like me, you love the book of Proverbs. Someone once said that it is "the Ten Commandments in shoe leather." It is a practical, down-to-earth guide for a life lived in covenant relationship with God. For many years, I read the book through on a monthly basis. But I never stopped to really study it, to analyze its nuances, or to make thoughtful application of its wisdom to every aspect of my life. Sound familiar?

PROVERBS FOR EVERYONE

In 1988 I began an in-depth study of Proverbs. I quickly realized that much of what had been written about Proverbs was written before this century. (I have listed a partial bibliography on page 8.) Using these and other commentaries, my study took over seven years and culminated in a soon-to-be published manuscript entitled *Proverbs for Everyone,* a 600-page devotional/study from which *Proverbs for Promise Keeping* is drawn.

PROVERBS FOR PROMISE KEEPING

This volume generally utilizes the topics and sequence of the book *Seven Promises of a Promise Keeper* (Focus on the Family: Colorado Springs, 1994). Each proverb has been selected to emphasize a particular aspect of the topic at hand. A general principle is then drawn, and a brief exposition follows. The examples from Scripture show the outcome of either obeying or disobeying the principle drawn. Finally, a short prayer makes a general application.

A personal action page follows each chapter subdivision. Questions are then posed for either group or individual study, other proverbs dealing with the topic are listed for further meditation, and a memory verse is proposed. At the bottom of the page there is space to write down a personal action plan to apply what has been learned. The lessons of Proverbs are valueless if not put into practical and consistent application in our lives.

THE "HARD CANDY" OF THE BIBLE

My pastor, George Miladin, likens the book of Proverbs to "hard candy." He says that the verses of Solomon's book are not to be chewed up quickly and swallowed, but rather turned over and over in the cheek. Their sweetness and wisdom should be allowed to glide slowly over the spiritual taste buds and savored, as we are given the Spirit's insight into how each verse is best applied to our lives. All I have attempted to do is to remove the wrapper from the candy. I hope that the pure sweetness of God's Word and the straight paths down which it will lead you will guide you all the days of your life.

Bob Beasley
San Diego, California

BIBLIOGRAPHY

Bridges, Charles. *A Commentary On Proverbs*. Carlisle, Pa.: Banner of Truth, 1846.

Ironside, H.A. *Proverbs/Song of Solomon*. Neptune, N.J.: Loizeaux Bros., 1908

Kidner, Derek. *Proverbs*. Downers Grove, Ill.: InterVarsity, 1975.

Lawson, George. *Commentary On Proverbs*. Grand Rapids, Mich.: Kregel, 1829.

·Chapter One·
A MAN AND HIS GOD

In this first chapter, we will investigate the relationship of a Christian man to his God. Understanding that the child of God is related to his heavenly Father by grace through faith alone, such saving faith manifests itself in several ways in the life of the Christian. Once born again to new life in Christ, a man is empowered from above to seek God's glory by conforming his life to the guidance of the Spirit of God.

Our Father loves us with a love that is beyond human understanding. He wants us to live joyful, successful lives; lives devoted to His kingdom and to His glory. The book of Proverbs gives us very practical instruction on how to do that on a day-by-day basis.

In our study, we will look at three means by which we express our relationship to God, and by which we are encouraged and strengthened in that relationship: Worship, Prayer, and God's Word.

·Chapter One·
A MAN AND HIS GOD

Part One:
Worship

Worship is the principal way in which we bring glory and honor to God. The old Ford Motor Company ad said that quality was their "Job 1." In other words, quality was their top priority. In the same way, worship is the Christian's "Job 1," and will be for all eternity. We have been created by God for God's glory, and our worship of Him is to be for His glory and for our everlasting joy.

The kind of worship we will be talking about is not our Sunday morning corporate worship service. Proverbs has little to say about group meetings. Rather, the proverbs will guide us inside our own hearts, to see the kinds of attitudes and motives that are there, and to show us those that please God. We will also learn something of who this God is whom we worship. It is of utmost importance that we worship the true God, and not some idol of our own making.

Worship God by Pursuing Righteousness

8) The Lord detests the sacrifice of the wicked, but the prayer of the upright pleases him. 9) The Lord detests the way of the wicked but he loves those who pursue righteousness.
(Prov. 15:8, 9)

A misconception among some professing Christians is that believing a set of facts about Jesus automatically brings eternal life. Others who profess Christ believe that baptism alone opens heaven's doors. Yet, many of these people continue to live without any evidence of the Spirit's leading to godliness. They have a form of godliness, but deny its power (2 Tim. 3:5).

John tells us that whoever claims to be a Christian must walk as Jesus did (1 John 2:6). This theme is repeated often in Scripture, even by the Lord Himself as in John 14:6. At the new birth, God's Spirit comes to reside in the heart of the believer. The Christian then seeks a life of righteousness by faith in the One who has given him eternal life. This is pleasing to God (Heb. 11:6), who accepts the prayers and worship of this righteous one. We are not righteous of ourselves, but only through faith in the One who shed His blood for us.

Scriptural Examples

Daniel. Daniel purposed in his heart not to defile himself before God. Through Gabriel, God told Daniel that both he and his prayers were highly esteemed (Dan. 9:23).

The Pharisee and the tax collector. The praying Pharisee commended himself but condemned the tax collector. But the tax collector confessed that he was a sinner, and begged for mercy. Jesus tells us that it was the tax collector who was justified before God (Luke 18:10-14).

Eunice and Lois. Paul commended Timothy's mother and grandmother for their sincere and active faith. They lived their faith, and taught young Timothy to do the same (2 Tim. 1:5).

Prayer of Application

Dear God, guide me in the paths of righteousness to which You have called me. May every thought be acceptable in Your sight, and may I worship You in spirit and in truth.

Beware of Superficiality in Worship

**To do what is right and just
is more acceptable to the Lord than sacrifice (Prov. 21:3).**

The Hebrew word here for "sacrifice" is *zebach*. In this case it clearly means the slaughter of an animal in ritual sacrifice. Animal sacrifices were established by God and were pleasing to Him (Gen. 4:4; 8:21). Yet Solomon is saying that there are things we can do that are much more pleasing to God.

The sacrifices established by God were to point to the great sacrifice of the Lord Jesus Christ. But they were detestable to Him if valued only for themselves and not for the One to whom they pointed; the righteous and just One. Righteousness and justice are the reality, while animal sacrifices were but a shadow of that reality (Heb. 10:1-2).

People throughout the ages have deceived themselves into thinking that mere superficial observance of some religious ritual can please God (Prov. 21:2). The practice of church sacraments without a corresponding and underlying true repentance and faith is detestable to God (Ps. 51:16, 17). What God demands is a living sacrifice! He wants your whole being! All of you! That is your acceptable worship (Rom. 12:1).

Scriptural Examples

The Pharisees and teachers of the law. These men were scathingly rebuked by Jesus for their superficiality. Our Lord raked them over the coals for neglecting the more weighty matters of justice, mercy, and faithfulness (Matt. 23:23).

Solomon. No man sacrificed more animals to God than this king of Israel. But underlying them were wisdom and the practice of justice and mercy in his kingdom (1 Kings 3:4; 8:64).

Cain. Cain brought a sacrifice to God, but it was superficial. God looked upon Cain's heart and saw that he had not brought his heart to the altar as his brother Abel had (Gen. 4:3-7).

Prayer of Application

Lord, I see much of the Pharisees' superficiality in myself. Forgive me and cleanse me from it. Help me to present my body daily as a living sacrifice to You for Your glory.

Beware of Worship Without Repentance

The sacrifice of the wicked is detestable – how much more so when brought with evil intent! (Prov. 21:27).

I am reminded of a scene in one of the "Godfather" movies where the Mob goes to church so that Robert DeNiro, who played the title role, could get baptized. Here he was, a man who earned his living breaking every commandment of God, being given the sign of God's covenant people. The very thought of such a thing is detestable to God, and particularly when it is done with evil intent such as the intent to deceive others in order to rob them. The Mob and their leader went out of the church and back to business as usual, raping and pillaging their community, selling drugs, and extorting money. They had made a mockery of the sacrament.

James says, "Religion that God our Father accepts as pure and faultless is this: to look after orphans and widows in their distress and to keep oneself from being polluted by the world" (James 1:27). David's prayer of confession states, "The sacrifices of God are a broken spirit; a broken and contrite heart" (Ps. 51:17). These are the sacrifices that are acceptable to God. Sacrifices, and hence worship, given without a corresponding change of heart in genuine repentance and turning from sin are detestable to God.

Scriptural Examples

Balaam. This wicked false prophet offered sacrifices to God. At the same time he conspired with Israel's enemy Balak to curse God's chosen people. What idiocy, to offer sacrifices with an evil intent. He did not get away with it (Num. 23:1-3, 13).

Absalom. This son of David offered animal sacrifices in Hebron after deceiving his father as to his evil intent. He really went to Hebron to establish himself as king over Israel, seeking to overthrow that which was instituted by God (2 Sam. 15:7-13).

Prayer of Application

Sovereign Lord, forgive me for the times I have tried to worship You with a heart hardened to You and to Your Word. Create in me a heart devoted to You in repentance and faith.

Worship the Lord with Rejoicing
**All the days of the oppressed are wretched,
but the cheerful heart has a continual feast (Prov. 15:15).**

The natural man's afflictions caused by his sin or the sin of others bring him only grief and bitterness. There is a sense in which the unsaved man never has a good day. Even on days when things seem to be going his way, he is only storing up wrath for himself against the day of God's wrath (Rom. 2:5).

Even though the Christian may go through difficult problems and circumstances, deep within there should be a peace and a joy that passes understanding (Phil. 4:7). There is a sense in which the Christian never has a bad day, as he knows that all things, even those circumstances that are hurtful and bitter at the time, are the work of his Sovereign Lord in his life. They are designed by God for his ultimate good (Rom. 8: 28, 29).

Therefore, Paul is able to say that whatever the circumstances that surround him, he has learned to be content (Phil. 4:11). And Nehemiah, when instructing the people, said that they should not grieve, for the joy of the Lord was their strength (Neh. 8:10). Ours is a joyful feast that will never end, thanks to the finished work of our Savior. Worship Him with rejoicing!

Scriptural Examples
Paul and Silas. In Thyatira, Paul and Silas were thrown into prison and put into stocks. But even locked up, they sang hymns to God, rejoicing in their afflictions (Acts 16:16-34).

Job. Stripped of his earthly possessions, and his children dead, Job praised his Lord anyway. Later, he said that even if the Lord killed him, yet would he trust Him (Job 1:21; 13:15).

Habakkuk. The prophet Habakkuk cried out that even if all the crops failed and the cattle died, yet he would rejoice in the Lord who was his strength. Oh, to have the faith of Habbakuk, giving thanks in all things (Hab. 3:17-19).

Prayer of Application
Our Father, help me to see the truth when I am going through trials in this life. Give me faith to trust You fully in these times of confusion, and to worship You with rejoicing.

Worship God in His Sovereignty
**The lot is cast into the lap,
but its every decision is from the Lord (Prov. 16:33).**

Some Christians think of God as a disinterested observer of this world. Others view Him as a sort of glorified errand boy who is waiting to serve their every whim. But the biblical picture of God is as Sovereign Lord, who is working out His purposes in the history of this planet in detail.

Historians can't tell us much about the "lot" in terms of what it looked like, but its purpose was to aid in making decisions. I've always envisioned a pair of dice when I hear the term "lot." The dice players in Las Vegas say, "Luck be a lady tonight." But the Bible teaches that there is no such thing as "luck."

While we do not know much about the lot, I think we have a better way today for good decision making. First, we should seek to *know the Word of God* (2 Peter 1:19). Then, *trust fully in the One who wrote it* (Prov. 3:5-6), resting in His providential care. Next, *seek the godly advice of others*. Finally, let's *make our decisions and step out by faith* in the sovereignty of the One who created and sustains all things by His powerful Word (Heb. 1:3). Worship God by resting in Him in faith.

Scriptural Examples
Joseph. He was cast into a pit by his brothers at precisely the same time a caravan of Ishmaelites went by. Joseph wound up as a slave in Egypt. Later, in power there, Joseph told his brothers that they had meant his slavery for evil, but God had intended it for good (Gen. 37:25; 45:4-8).

Jonah. The sailors on the ship carrying Jonah cast lots to see who was responsible for the storm that threatened their ship. The lot fell upon Jonah, so they cast him into the sea at precisely the same time that a great fish, which God had prepared, swam by and swallowed him. Luck? No way (Jonah1:7).

Prayer of Application
Father, help me always to rest in You. Your power to control every detail of Your creation is too high for me to understand, but by faith I can find my rest in it, and please You.

Worship God in Intimate Fellowship

**31) Do not envy a violent man or choose any of his ways,
32) for the Lord detests a perverse man
but takes the upright into his confidence (Prov. 3:31-32).**

The chasm that separates the natural man from his Creator is extremely wide and deep, and no one can cross it on his own (Luke 16: 26). Only by the Lord making us "upright" can we be reunited in friendship with a Holy God. A similar gulf exists between the ways of the man who follows God's wisdom and the man who does violence to it (Ezek. 22:26).

Christians are dead to sin and to the ways of the violent man, but alive unto intimate fellowship with God, the most wonderful treasure imaginable. We have His close friendship (John 15:13); communion (John 14:21-23); peace (Phil. 4:6-7); joy (Neh. 8:10); assurance (Rev. 2:17); instruction (Matt. 11:25); confidence (John 15:15); providence (Ps.107:43); and all the blessings of His eternal covenant with us (Ps. 25:14) (Bridges, p. 40).

In Psalm 51:11-12, David cries out for God to restore him to the joy of his salvation. Sin breaks our intimacy with God, even though He still loves us as His children. If you find that the sweet fellowship between you and God has been interrupted, search your heart for the sin that has done it, confess it and turn from it. Then you will return to that sweet and intimate friendship with the Creator and Sustainer of the universe.

Scriptural Examples

David and Goliath. What a contrast between these two men. Goliath was a violent bully, prideful and arrogant. David, a shepherd boy, dared to stand up to him, killing Goliath with one well-placed stone. While David would later become known as a man of violence (1 Chron. 22:8), he nevertheless enjoyed an intimate confidence with God, and penned many wonderful Psalms attesting to it.

Prayer of Application

Sweet Lord, You have lifted me up from the mire and placed my feet upon a rock. Keep me in intimate fellowship with You, Lord, as I seek to serve and worship You, glorifying Your name.

My Personal Action Plan

STUDY QUESTIONS

1. In the second of the Ten Commandments, God forbade the worship of idols, which are no more than impotent substitutes for the true God. We do not see many people bowing down to wooden statues in America today, but other idols abound. Which of these might you call an impotent god in our society? (a) Material possessions, (b) Drugs, (c) Sex, (d) Entertainment, (e) False 'gospels' such as Mormonism and Jehovah's Witnesses, the new age and the occult, (f) Sports stars.

2. Exodus 34:14 gives God's name as "Jealous." Why is God jealous? Of whom is He jealous? For whom is He jealous?

3. In Psalm 95:1-7, how many reasons can you find to worship the Lord? Then, in 95:8, what do you think it means to "harden your heart"? Have you ever hardened your heart?

4. In Matthew 15:8-9, Jesus, quoting Isaiah, makes some very severe judgments against the religious leaders of His day. What had they done to deserve such condemnation?

5. Read Romans 12:1-20. What does Paul see as our "spiritual act of worship"? In verse 2, what specifically are we to do?

PROVERBS TO PONDER
3:5, 6; 8:14-16; 8:22-31; 15:3; 16:1; 16:9

ONE TO MEMORIZE
There is no wisdom, no insight, no plan that can succeed against the Lord (Prov. 21:30).

MAKING APPLICATION
My personal action plan to worship God in spirit and in truth:

1 _____ 2 _____

3 _____ 4 _____

.Chapter One.
A MAN AND HIS GOD
....

Part Two:
Prayer

Prayer is what we do to communicate with God. It is an important exercise of our faith, perhaps the most important. I like to think of prayer as a kind of thermometer of faith. Little faith means little prayer, while real faith is shown in believing in prayer. Each Friday morning, some men of our church meet for breakfast and prayer. If an unbeliever happened to be there, he would probably think we were speaking to our feet. But we are really speaking to an unseen Guest. How do we know He is with us and listening to us? We know it by faith, because He has promised it in His Word (Matt. 18:20).

One of God's designs for the book of Proverbs is to aid the man of God in his aim to be "conformed to the likeness of [God's] Son" (Rom. 8:29). Prayer is a chief part of that journey. In prayer, we pour out our hearts to God, we praise Him and give Him thanks. In short, in prayer we worship God with words, actively attributing to Him His eternal attributes of omniscience, love, and power.

Pray to Your Father Who Hears You

The Lord is far from the wicked,
but he hears the prayer of the righteous (Prov. 15:29).

God's presence fills the universe, so in that sense He is equally near every person on the planet (Acts 17:27-28). But in His gracious favor, He hears and answers the prayers of believers. At the crucifixion of Jesus, the curtain of the temple was torn in two (Matt. 27:51) and the way into God's presence was opened for us. What a great privilege we have in prayer!

Our duty as Christians is to pray always (1 Thess. 5:17). Our heavenly Father will not bar access to His seeking child. Rather, He is only too willing to give us the things we ask of Him, in His timing, and in accordance with His will. But let your prayers have a definite object in mind. Then, make sure your motives are right, and that you are not praying selfishly to bring yourself pleasure, with no profit for others or for God. Finally, have full confidence in the One who hears and responds. The prayer of faith is powerful and effective (James 5:17).

Scriptural Examples

The Israelites. The Lord turned a deaf ear to the people of Israel following their decision at Kadesh Barnea to fight the Amorites in their own strength. God would not bless their works done in the flesh (Deut. 1:45).

David. David testified that the Lord had heard his prayer and had delivered him from trouble (Ps. 116:1-7).

The enemies of David. David praised the Lord for deliverance and recounted how his enemies and Saul prayed to the Lord but were not heard (Ps. 18:40, 41).

The saints who prayed for Paul. Paul was delivered from sickness and death, and gave testimony to the effectiveness of the prayers of the saints who stood with him, and to the graciousness of the Lord in answering them (2 Cor. 1:9-11).

Prayer of Application

Father, teach me what it means to pray in faith, persistently believing that You will answer my prayer. Create in me a prayerful spirit, that I will thankfully bring all things to You.

Seek God in Your Daily Quiet Time

32) Now then, my sons, listen to me; blessed are those who keep my ways. 33) Listen to my instruction and be wise; do not ignore it. 34) Blessed is the man who listens to me, watching daily at my doors, waiting at my doorway. 35) For whoever finds me finds life and receives favor from the Lord. 36) But whoever fails to find me harms himself; all who hate me love death (Prov. 8:32-36).

Jesus said in Luke 9:23, "If anyone would come after me, he must deny himself and take up his cross daily and follow me." In Galatians 2:20, Paul says that we have been crucified with Christ, and we no longer live unto ourselves. Christ has become the central focus and purpose of the Christian's new life, a life that is lived by faith in Him. We can bear our cross only by faith, and we are to live moment by moment in it, from faith to faith, step by step, on a daily basis (Rom. 1:17).

These verses state two of the great blessings that have been promised to the person who will listen to the instruction of God's wisdom and keep God's ways. He will find *life* and *favor* (grace) from the Lord. These come by watching daily at His feet and waiting at His doorway (Rev. 3:20).

Those who say "I'm too busy" or "I don't have the time" to meet with God are really saying "My priorities don't allow time for You today, Lord." If your earthly boss asked for a 30-minute meeting each morning, could you find the time? Just as we need food daily to meet our physical needs (Matt. 6:11), so also do we need our daily feeding from the Vine of spiritual food. Without it, you will be a frail and fruitless Christian.

Scriptural Examples

The Bereans. The Bereans examined the Scriptures to see if what Paul said was true. What's more, the Scripture tells us that they did it on a daily basis (Acts 17:11).

Prayer of Application

Dear Lord, who provides all things richly for our enjoyment, help me to recognize You as the giver of all things, and to make time for prayer and for Your Word on a daily basis.

Cry Out to God for His Wisdom

1) My son, if you accept my words and store up my commands within you, 2) turning your ear to wisdom and applying your heart to understanding, 3) and if you call out for insight and cry aloud for understanding, 4) and if you look for it as silver and search for it as for hidden treasure, 5) then you will understand the fear of the Lord and find the knowledge of God (Prov. 2:1-5).

These verses are a treasure map for the greatest treasure imaginable. The directional arrows are the verbs found in these verses. Notice them. First, the treasure hunter needs to *accept* wisdom's words (1a). The serious student will diligently study God's Word and receive it by faith as truth. Next, he is to *store up* commandments within him (1b). He is to hide the Word in his heart (Ps. 119:11). Then, the student of the Word *turns his ear* to wisdom (2a), and *applies his heart* to understanding (2b). This is not academic research, but a spiritual quest. Then in verse 3, we find the student on his knees *crying out* in prayer for understanding and insight (James 1:5). Finally (4), he keeps on *looking* and *searching* for it as hidden treasure (Matt. 7:7).

And what is the treasure that the student so diligently seeks? It is to know the One True God. And how shall we know Him? We will find that His name is Jesus, who is the same "El Shaddai" and "Yahweh" of fearsome majesty. He is our shield, and our exceeding great reward (Gen. 15:1). He is the treasure, hidden from the world (2 Cor. 4:3-4), but revealed to those who would seek Him in His Word and in prayer. He is, in fact, wisdom personified. (Prov. 8; 1 Cor. 1:30).

Scriptural Examples

Daniel. Here is a man who knew the fearsome majesty of his God, and yet had an intimate personal relationship with his treasure, who was his God. When men came to see him, they found him in prayer, calling out to his God for help (Dan. 6:11).

Prayer of Application

Father, how I want to know Jesus, to fix my thoughts upon Him and find the treasure of joy that He has for me. Dear God, supply me with the wisdom that can only be found in Christ.

Find Strength in the Lord Your Refuge

**He who fears the Lord has a secure fortress,
and for his children it will be a refuge (Prov. 14:26).**

How can "fear" and "security" operate together? We usually think of them as opposites. Fear would normally mean lack of security, and vice versa. Here, however, we are told that the fear of the Lord leads to the security of a fortress. The answer lies in our understanding of the phrase "the fear of the Lord." This is not the fear that perfect love casts out (1 John 4:18), but the fear that love brings in. It is the reverence that a child has for his father, prompting him to obey his father regardless of the circumstances. Fear of the Lord is taking delight in what God commands us to do (Ps. 112:1). We *fear* the Lord, but we are not *afraid* of the Lord. His fear in us gives us boldness and strength, and, in fact, strong confidence and security. We find such confidence in bold and faithful prayer.

When we were not yet God's children, we fled from His presence. Some of us hid in alcohol, some in religion, some in our work, some in our insane denial of His very existence. But now, by His grace, we flee toward Him in prayer and intimacy. God is our refuge and strength (Ps. 46:1). Even in the face of death we have confidence in Him as our ultimate refuge.

Scriptural Examples

Abraham. When God commanded Abraham to take Isaac to Mt. Moriah and offer him as a sacrifice, the two set out in fear, yet in faith. Abraham, in his fear of God, knew that even if he were required to sacrifice Isaac, God had the power to raise his son from the dead (Gen. 22:2-14; Heb.11:17-19).

Stephen. As the Sanhedrin began to stone him, Stephen looked to heaven and saw his refuge opened before him. He expressed confidence in his heavenly advocate, Jesus, whom he saw standing at the right hand of the Father (Acts 7:55-60).

Prayer of Application

Father, I thank You that because of Jesus' finished work on the cross, where He reconciled me to You, I have found refuge from my fear of death. Help me to find a daily refuge in You.

Pray for God's Control over Your Life

7) Two things I ask of you, O Lord; do not refuse me before I die: 8) Keep falsehood and lies far from me; give me neither poverty nor riches, but give me only my daily bread.
9) Otherwise, I may have too much and disown you and say, 'Who is the Lord?' Or, I may become poor and steal, and so dishonor the name of my God (Prov. 30:7-9).

A man named Agur penned these verses. Because he says in verse 7, "before I die," it seems to me that this was Agur's "life prayer." Do you have a "life prayer" like you may have a "life verse"? If not, you might want to adopt Agur's. He asks for only two things. First, he asks to be kept from falsehood and lies. The world system is a system of lies, of self-seeking deception. It says it will do what only God can do and leads many astray. How different is God's way, the way of humility and truth. Agur is a man of humility and we see it clearly in his prayer.

The second part of Agur's prayer is strange indeed. How many folks do you know who pray that they may be kept from riches? Not many I'm sure. Most of us see riches as a blessing of God. But Agur knew that often the more material wealth a man has, the less he thinks he needs God. Then in verse 8 he asks that he also be kept from poverty. He feared he would become a thief under those circumstances.

Agur wants simply to bring honor to the name of his God (9b). This should be the motivating force behind every Christian's life (1 Cor. 10:31; Phil. 2:11). Each of us should pray that God will control every detail of our lives, then submit fully to His providential care. That is the need of every Christian.

Scriptural Examples

Jeshurun. The name "Jeshurun" is a pseudonym for Israel. In Deuteronomy 32:15 we find that Jeshurun grew fat and sleek and was filled with food. He abandoned God his Savior, which is exactly what Agur had feared in his prayer.

Prayer of Application

Lord, I want to adopt Agur's prayer as my own. I have seen what riches can do to people, and I'm afraid of that prospect. Control every part of my life, that I might walk in Your ways.

Beware of Mocking God
If anyone turns a deaf ear to the law,
even his prayers are detestable (Prov. 28:9).

Prayer is an unspeakable privilege. As those words flow from my fingers to the computer screen, I am shivering inside. Oh, that I were more a man of prayer. I must confess that I am not nearly what I should be. But I know that when I pray, God is faithful to hear and answer my prayer because I revere His law and try to apply it consistently to my life. Do I always do so? No, sadly I do not, but I *want* to (Rom. 7:15-21).

This proverb addresses the man who will not even listen to the law of God. That is, he will not open God's Word and read it, and then prayerfully seek to make it the grid through which all his thoughts, words, and actions are judged. In short, he couldn't care less about what God has to say, although ironically he thinks God should care about what he has to say. He wants the benefits of knowing God with none of the responsibility. The prayers of such a one are detestable to God.

Are you like the person who turns a deaf ear to God? If so, you might like to know of the exception to the rule of the proverb above. God will hear the prayer of the repentant heart. Confess your idolatry to God and He will hear from heaven and forgive you (1 Kings 8:33-39; 2 Chron. 7:14).

Scriptural Examples

Simon the sorcerer. This man was practicing witchcraft in Samaria when he heard the gospel through Phillip. When Peter and John came up from Jerusalem, Simon, wishing to use the Holy Spirit as a tool to increase his sorcery business, offered to pay the apostles for the gift of the Spirit. Peter saw through his idolatry and rebuked him (Acts 8:9-24).

The elders of Israel. These men came to Ezekiel to seek the Lord. The Lord would not allow them to inquire of Him because the idolatry of their fathers was continuing (Ezek. 20).

Prayer of Application

Dear God, thank You for the privilege of prayer. Help me, Lord, to be a man of much prayer. But I understand that if I won't listen to You and Your law, neither will You listen to me.

My Personal Action Plan
....

STUDY QUESTIONS

1. Which of the following is your favorite excuse for not praying with intensity and consistency? (Skip this one if you do pray hard and often.)

   a. I just don't have the time.
   b. I'm too tired when I get home.
   c. God is sovereign. He's got everything worked out, and I won't change His mind.
   d. _____ (Fill in your own.)

2. Read 2 Chronicles 7:14. What are the four things that God's people must do in order for God to hear and answer them?

3. In light of Job 42:8, should we ask others whom we know are walking with God to pray for us? Do you consider it a privilege to pray for others?

4. Why do you suppose Jesus commanded that we pray in secret and not as those who prayed in public places (Matt. 6:5-6)?

5. Look at Luke 18:1-8. What does this teaching of Jesus tell us about persistence in prayer?

6. Paul asked God to take away a "thorn" in his flesh, yet God refused. Does this mean God didn't answer Paul (2 Cor. 12:7-9)?

PROVERBS TO PONDER
1:22-33; 15:8; 19:3; 21:13

ONE TO MEMORIZE
The Lord is far from the wicked
but he hears the prayer of the righteous (Prov. 15:29).

MAKING APPLICATION
My personal action plan to become a consistent prayer warrior:

1)_____ 2)_____

3)_____ 4)_____

.Chapter One.
A MAN AND HIS GOD

Part Three:
God's Word

The Bible is the medium through which God speaks to us. His Holy Spirit makes the Bible lessons real when we adopt its teachings and commandments as the ruling influences over our lives. It is our only source for faith and practice. Through the Bible, we know who God is, and that He is trustworthy and powerful, the God of ultimate love, yet also the God of ultimate wrath. He is the God of our salvation (Ps. 27:1; 62:6).

The Word of God, from its beginning in Genesis to its end in Revelation, is the story of the Living Word, the Alpha and Omega, the Lord Jesus Christ. It is a book that the man of God is called to master (2 Tim. 2:15).

The relationship between a man and his Bible is crucial in the Christian life. When I was a new Christian, I heard someone say, "You can tell a good local church by the fact that people are carrying their Bibles into it." That was good advice. But I have found that it is not enough just to carry one's Bible into the church building. The Bible is like a diamond mine. It is of no value unless you get into it and get your knees dirty.

Apply Yourself to Study the Bible
**Apply your heart to instruction
and your ears to words of knowledge (Prov. 23:12).**

Lately I've been reading into the many and varied religions and cults in America. It is amazing how many different "gospels" there are today. How do we know that we have the right one? How do we know for sure that salvation is by faith alone in Christ Jesus? We can know for sure by adhering to this proverb, and applying our hearts to the instruction and knowledge of God's Word.

Few Christians regularly dwell in the Word, particularly the Old Testament. Some pay attention to the pastor's sermon on Sunday, and some may join a Bible study or attend Sunday school. But in many of today's churches, laypeople have given up rigorous Bible study, deferring to the seminary-trained "professional." I thank God for our evangelical seminaries, and for those who have undergone their godly disciplines. But the Bible deals with matters of eternal consequence, and I want to know the truth for myself. Furthermore, if you and I are to grow in Christ, we need to know the Word and to put it into practice every day (Heb. 5:11-14).

Each Christian, by the illumination of the Holy Spirit, can be like the Bereans of Paul's day who "examined the Scriptures every day to see if what Paul said was true" (Acts 17:11). Indeed, it is our responsibility before God (2 Tim. 2:15).

Scriptural Examples
Ezra. This man had God's gracious hand upon him because he devoted himself to the study and observance of the law of the Lord, and taught others to do the same (Ezra 7:10).

Apollos. We're told in Acts of this man's knowledge of the Old Testament. He was a great help to many in the early church, and is mentioned often by Paul (Acts 18:24, 27; 1 Cor. 3-4).

Prayer of Application
Lord, You have given us Your Word so that we may know of Your power and trustworthiness. Give me a hunger for Your Word and a thirst for the righteousness that is mine through it.

Trust Every Word of God

**5) Every word of God is flawless; he is a shield to those
who take refuge in him. 6) Do not add to his words,
or he will rebuke you and prove you a liar (Prov. 30:5-6).**

Satan's prime target is the Christian's trust in the sufficiency and trustworthiness of the Bible. Many either deny the
Bible's trustworthiness by denying its verbal inspiration by the
Holy Spirit, or deny the Bible's sufficiency by adding human
words to the very words of God. God will rebuke these people
and prove them to be liars.

Agur, who wrote these verses, believed in the Word of God.
He says in verse 5 that "every Word of God is flawless." Those
of us who flee to God and His Word for refuge find that He is
trustworthy to shield us from the ultimate tragedy of eternal
judgment. He provides for our future security and His words
are able to make us wise unto that salvation (2 Tim. 3:15).

In verse 6 above, Agur speaks of the sufficiency of Scripture. Many would add to the words of God by other writings
and by their traditions. The Jews in Jesus' day were guilty of
this error by their Talmud, or oral tradition, which they held to
be equal with God's Word. Jesus told them on one instance,
"You nullify the Word of God for the sake of your tradition"
(Matt. 15:6). Today, the Roman Catholic church has a body of
tradition by which God's Word is erroneously augmented. For
example, they teach of a place called "purgatory," which has no
biblical basis. When people do this, they deny that the Scripture
is sufficient (2 Tim. 3:16-17).

Scriptural Examples

Satan. Behind all the Bible-bashing in the world is Satan. In
the garden, he first tempted Eve by questioning the truth of
God's Word. Do not follow him. Follow God by trusting in His
perfect Word that He has provided for your refuge (Gen. 3:1-6).

Prayer of Application

Lord, thank You for the trustworthiness and sufficiency of
the Bible. Help me to read it in sincerity and faith, seeking to do
what it says, enjoying its refuge and its sure salvation.

Love the Commandments of Christ

1) My son, keep my words and store up my commands within you. 2) Keep my commands and you will live; guard my teachings as the apple of your eye. 3) Bind them on your fingers; write them on the tablet of your heart. 4) Say to wisdom, "You are my sister," and call understanding your kinsman; 5) they will keep you from the adulteress, from the wayward wife with her seductive words (Prov. 7:1-5).

In verse 2 here, Solomon uses the phrase, "the apple of your eye." I heard that phrase often while growing up. It always described something or someone that was adored. God uses it in that sense in Deuteronomy 32:9-11 in describing Israel, whom He kept under the shadow of His wing.

Jesus said, "If you love me, you will obey what I command" (John 14:15). We are told to love God and to love our neighbor, as these are the two commandments upon which all the others rest (Matt. 22:37-40). Should we not also love the commandments that He gives us to keep? But how are we to do this?

When you love something or someone, you'll want to spend time in that activity or with that person, and get to know all you can about the object of your love. So it is with Christ's commandments. How can we love them if we don't know them? Christ says in effect, "Love me, love my commandments." Study them until, like the Psalmist, you can say, "For I delight in your commands because I love them" (Ps. 119:47).

Scriptural Examples

The lover. In Solomon's "Song of Songs" he describes a lover as an apple tree. Delight is found in its shade and its fruit is sweet to the taste. A man takes a maiden to a banquet, and his banner over her is love. Likewise, what a Husband and Lover we have in the Lord Jesus Christ, who sits us down to feast at His eternal table under the banner of His love. Love Christ and His commandments (Song 2:3-6).

Prayer of Application

Lord Jesus, thank You for Your protecting banner of love over me. May I in turn live for You, and in living love You and Your wonderful commandments for me.

Let the Word of God Sink In

The wise in heart accept commands,
but a chattering fool comes to ruin (Prov. 10:8).

At one time I was in the home building business in California and Florida. Soil conditions, which are important in designing foundations for homes, vary widely. Compaction tests determine the soil's ability to bear weight. Drainage is necessary to carry water away from the foundations. Percolation measures the ability of the soil to drain water vertically into the ground.

In Florida, the sandy soils on which I built homes percolated water so fast that the soils-engineer's instruments could not measure it. But in southern California, where the composition of the soil tends to be decomposed granite and clay, percolation may be very, very slow.

Men's hearts are like soils, as we're told by Jesus in Luke 8:5-8. Some hearts receive the Word and, like water on sand, it sinks deep. This person grows in the Word and becomes sound in the faith. He becomes obedient to the indwelling Word.

The chattering fool is just the opposite. He may be continually exposed to the Word, but it runs off his mind without ever getting to his heart. He may even chatter on about creeds and doctrines and theology, but without any real evidence in his life of the indwelling presence of the Word as applied by the Spirit. As the proverb anticipates, such a man will come to ruin.

Scriptural Examples

The Thessalonians. Paul thanked God for those who had received the Word of God, which had gone to work in their hearts through faith (1 Thess. 2:13).

Diotrephes. This malicious person, a chattering fool, was opposing the apostle John and refusing even to welcome brothers in the faith. John said that his evil actions indicated that he had not seen God (3 John 9-11).

Prayer of Application

Dear Lord, thank You for godly men like my pastors, who feed me with the truth of Your Word. But hearing isn't enough. Help me to allow the Word to penetrate deep into my soul.

Let God's Word Purify Your Thoughts

**The Lord detests the thoughts of the wicked,
but those of the pure are pleasing to him (Prov. 15:26).**

The secret place of the mind, where plans are devised and where secret sins are harbored, is not really secret at all but is laid wide open before the Lord, to whom all men must give account (Heb. 4:13). The natural man has shut God out of his thinking, and his heart has become darkened (Rom. 1:21). That man's thoughts are detested by God, no matter how righteous the man himself may think they are.

But for the child of God, who by the grace of God has received salvation through faith in Christ, the Holy Spirit invades his heart through the medium of his mind and begins a process of purification (Rom.12:2). How does it happen?

When snails are readied for the table, they are taken from their natural setting and fed only corn meal or another such pure food. Over time, their flesh loses its wild taste and becomes purified and cleansed. Similarly, the Christian is called to feed upon God's Word, which can cleanse and purify the thoughts, words, and way of the man of God (Ps. 119:9).

Scriptural Examples

The pre-Flood generation. God saw that the pre-Flood heart and thoughts of man were only wicked. These men and women followed the abominable thought patterns of their forefather, Cain, and gave expression to them in violent ways. God sent the flood waters to destroy them from the face of the earth. Only the godly Noah and his family survived, and that only by the grace of their Creator God (Gen. 6:5).

Tychicus. Paul commended his brother Tychicus to the church at Ephesus, knowing that he would encourage all the saints there and speak to them words of comfort, which flowed from the pure thoughts of his heart (Eph. 6:21-22).

Prayer of Application

Heavenly Father, put a real desire in my heart for holiness. I pray that the Holy Spirit purifying me through the Word might transform me into the man You want me to be.

Be Strongly Grounded in Your Faith

A simple man believes anything,
but a prudent man gives thought to his steps (Prov. 14:15).

The Christian faith is not a blind faith. It is a faith based on solid historic fact that is backed up by the testimony of eye-witnesses and millions of believers down through the centuries. It is a faith grounded in truth that was recorded in God's Word over thousands of years by various authors, yet with one basic message and no contradictions or errors. Furthermore, the Bible has a quality called "perspicuity." That is, its basic doctrines are essentially clear and understandable by anyone who wants to diligently study it and seek its truth (2 Tim. 3:16).

The simple man is tossed to and fro by every wind of doctrine and by the cunning craftiness of deceitful men (Eph. 4:14). Be careful not to let this happen to you. Prayerfully ground your faith in the lifelong study of the Word. It is a book that is sufficient for life and doctrine, and does not need any other book or priesthood to interpret it. Consider carefully each doctrine you hear and discern whether or not it is true by testing it against the revealed word of God. Be cautious of the teachers you follow and of the church you join. Build your profession of faith on the solid rock of God's Word, not on the shifting sand of another person's opinion (Matt. 7:24-27).

Scriptural Examples

Eve. Acting out of emotion and self-will, rather than of faith in what God had said, Eve was beguiled by Satan and ate the forbidden fruit. Her rebellion started, as rebellion always does, with a questioning of the revealed Word of God (Gen. 3:1-6).

Timothy. Paul commended Timothy, who from infancy had known the Holy Scriptures. Those Scriptures are able to make one wise unto salvation and are useful in equipping every man for God's purposes (2 Tim. 3:14-17).

Prayer of Application

Father, how I love Your Word, which is trustworthy and true and sufficient, and which is profitable in all ways for my life and walk with You. Help me to be firmly established in it.

My Personal Action Plan

STUDY QUESTIONS

1. The following are all potential results of consistent Bible study. How would you rank each on a scale of 0 to 10?

    a. Be able to amaze your friends with your knowledge of the Scriptures.

    b. Become a mature Christian brother on whom others can count in times of trial and affliction.

    c. Become more like Christ in His obedience.

    d. Feel superior to other denominations.

    e. Be able to instruct others in the Word.

    f. Increase your faith through knowledge of the Word.

2. What time of the day do you find most conducive to personal Bible reading and study? Why?

3. In light of 2 Timothy 2:15, in what ways would a person be ashamed because he had neglected Bible study?

4. Read Hebrews 4:12-13. In what way is the Word of God living? Why would it be compared to a sword?

5. In Ephesians 6:17, the Word is again compared to a sword. How is this sword different from that in Hebrews? (Hint: Study the contexts of the two "sword" verses.)

6. Psalm 119:11 provides what secret to obedience?

PROVERBS TO PONDER
4:20-22; 13:13; 14:6; 19:27; 20:27; 22:12

ONE TO MEMORIZE
Every word of God is flawless;
he is a shield to those who take refuge in him (Prov. 30:5).

MAKING APPLICATION
My personal action plan to become a student of the Word of God:

1)_____   2)_____

3)_____   4)_____

.Chapter *Two*.
A MAN AND HIS MENTORS

In the last chapter, we studied three ways in which we relate directly to our Heavenly Father. In this chapter, we will look at three interactions by which we are assisted in our relationship with God: mentoring relationships with others, God's discipline over us, and our relationship to our parents.

The Christian life is never lived in isolation from people. In fact, it is in our daily interaction with others, both believers and unbelievers, that we act out our faith, and through which we grow in righteousness and understanding. Theoretically, we could follow the demands of God for worship, prayer, and Bible study on a desert island, all alone. But God's plan for His people involves family, church, and local society. Not surprisingly, He has provided counselors for us to help shape our lives in these communities, to His glory.

.Chapter Two.
A MAN AND HIS MENTORS

Part One:
Mentoring Relationships

There is an old secular proverb which is always rendered in a thick German accent: "Ve get too soon oldt, undt too late schmart." Life on this planet is short and getting more complex by the hour. We are finite and fallen and we don't have all the answers. To think that we do is the height of arrogance. Every one of us needs help in all kinds of ways, and God has provided that help if we'll only look around us. Christian brothers come in all sizes, shapes, ages, and colors, and with assorted backgrounds, training, gifts, and levels of understanding. We have this one thing in common: we all love the Lord Jesus Christ and want to serve Him. In loving the Lord we love one another and we should seek to serve each other. One area of that service is in discipleship. One of the outstanding principles of Promise Keepers is its emphasis on the value of personal mentoring relationships. Each of us needs a Paul, a Barnabas, and a Timothy. In other words, we all need someone to mentor us, someone to whom we can be accountable and share our innermost needs, and finally, someone for whom we can provide mentorship.

Brothers, Disciple One Another

**As iron sharpens iron,
so one man sharpens another (Prov. 27:17).**

Back in 1980, a friend of mine and I began a businessmen's Bible study. Recently, a young man joined our study. One morning he told us why he had come. "I just like the openness of this group," he said. "I feel free to share my troubles and heartaches here and to receive help from teaching, prayer, and godly advice." This is foundational in the Christian life: teaching and encouraging one another (Col. 3:16; 1 Thess. 5:11).

The Christian life needs to be lived in intimate fellowship with others who share our precious faith. The writer to the Hebrews enjoins us to "encourage one another daily," to the end that "none of you may be hardened by sin's deceitfulness" (Heb. 3:13). This can be done neither in the context of a "loner" mentality nor that of a large group. There has to be personal intimacy, and this is only possible in the small group or in one-on-one discipling relationships.

If you are not involved in a small group or discipling ministry of some kind, I urge you to get involved. The only requirement is to be serious about living for and glorifying the Lord Jesus, and a consequent desire to be sharpened in your walk with God, and to sharpen others.

Scriptural Examples

Job. Eliphaz the Temanite spoke of his friend Job's discipling ministry. Job's words had supported those who had stumbled, and had strengthened those who had faltering knees (Job 4:3-4).

The men on the Emmaus Road. After the crucifixion, two men were walking from Jerusalem to Emmaus when a stranger appeared and spoke to them about the prophecies that had been fulfilled in Christ. Later, they recognized the stranger as the Lord Jesus, who had just discipled them (Luke 24:13).

Prayer of Application

Father God, thank You for my brothers in Christ, who share common experiences on the road of faith. Help me to take seriously my responsibility to encourage and disciple others.

Get Advice from Many Sources
For lack of guidance a nation falls,
but many advisers make victory sure (Prov. 11:14).

In seeking advice, there is a temptation to seek only the advice we will like. But the idea of advice is not to confirm our thinking, it is to establish our thinking. We seek advice from several perspectives. In doing so, we are able to uncover the blind spots in our own thoughts that are not apparent to us.

In forming a board of directors for a corporation, different disciplines are sought in board members because they will all approach decision making from different angles. From a team of diverse counselors, a business can establish a foundation that will chart a profitable and safe course through today's competitive environment.

We each need to seek counsel from many sources. Have a friend play "devil's advocate." Look for the downside potential of any course of action. Seek professional counsel. Whatever the decision to be made, the chances for it to be a right decision increase in direct relation to the solid advice one receives.

Scriptural Examples

King Rehoboam. Solomon's son chose to follow the advice of his friends and to scourge the people, rather than showing them kindness as his father's counselors advised. His problem was not that he didn't seek advice, but that he rejected the best advice and followed his own selfish motives. Because of his decision, the division of Israel ensued (1 Kings 12:6-19).

Ahab. This king of Israel sought advice about going to war. His 400 "yes" men all told him to go. But Jehoshaphat suggested that Ahab listen to Micaiah, the prophet of the Lord. Micaiah said he could only give God's advice, and that defeat awaited Ahab and his army. The lesson? Even if hundreds stand against the revealed will of God, choose His Word! (1 Kings 22:1-38).

Prayer of Application

Dear Lord, as I make decisions that affect my walk with You, help me to remember to seek out godly counsel. Thank You for men who will give me honest and competent advice.

Submit to the Rebuke of Wise Men
A mocker resents correction;
he will not consult the wise (Prov. 15:12).

The mocker's big problem is that he is full of rationalizations and self love. He has flattered himself for so long that he is unable to receive any criticism or rebuke which seeks to tear away his carefully constructed facade. The wise man who would tell him the truth is no friend, but an enemy (Gal. 4:15, 16). The mocker will avoid the light of truth at all costs (John 3:20). This is why the Word of God is so despised by the world. It sheds light upon the darkness of men's hearts (John 3:19).

As Christians, we need to seek the faithful rebuke of our righteous brothers so that we will continue to walk in the light. Each Christian should be accountable in each detail of his life to at least one other Christian so that sin may not be allowed to gain the slightest foothold (Heb. 3:12-13). At the same time, we need to study, meditate upon, and memorize the Word of God, which is able to instruct us in the way of righteousness so that we will be furnished for every good work (2 Tim. 3:17).

Scriptural Examples
The Israelites. At Kadesh Barnea, two of the twelve spies (Joshua and Caleb) who had gone in to look at the Promised Land exhorted the Israelites to go in and, by faith, take it. The people instead rebelled against their wisdom and sought to stone the pair (Num. 14:6-10).

Herodias. John the Baptist rebuked Herod for living with his brother's wife, Herodias. This mocker was so incensed by this rebuke that she sought John's murder (Mark 6:19).

The Pharisees. Jesus rebuked the Pharisees for their love of money and for justifying themselves in the eyes of men. They sneered at His reproof and later brought about His death on a Roman cross (Luke 16:13-15).

Prayer of Application
Heavenly Father, grant me the grace to seek out and act upon godly rebuke from Christian brothers. And help me to ingest Your Holy Word so that sin might not gain a foothold.

Go to Battle Armed with Good Advice

**Make plans by seeking advice;
if you wage war, obtain guidance (Prov. 20:18).**

In my lifetime, I have seen our U. S. Presidents struggle often with decisions when war hung in the balance. I am sure that any such decision is an agonizing one, and only made after the counsel of many advisers. I personally would not want to be faced with the responsibility of sending young men and women into armed conflict.

But every Christian is engaged in spiritual warfare (Phil. 1:30), and so I see this proverb in that light. Each Christian needs to establish his personal strategy in the struggle against Satan and his minions who would make war with God. We should do this armed with godly counsel and advice. There are as many different roles in the battle as there are soldiers. Some will fight in foxholes along the front lines, while others will be engaged in supplying the front line troops with bread, prayer, and encouragement.

Each one's calling in the battle plan will be in accordance with the gifts God has given him and should be established in the counsel of the Word of God. It should also be in the counsel of the wise advice of our pastors, elders, and other mature warriors of the faith.

Scriptural Examples

David. At war with the Philistines, David sought the counsel of God as to whether or not to attack. God said that he should, so David attacked and was victorious. But then the enemy entered the Valley of Rephaim. David once more inquired of God. This time, the Lord gave him tactical instructions: David was to circle around behind enemy lines, and as soon as he heard the sound of marching, he was to attack. David defeated the Philistines again (2 Sam. 5:17-25).

Prayer of Application

Father, You have drafted me into spiritual warfare. Help me to take up Your battle cry and, armed with advice from Your Word and godly men, pitch daily into the fray.

Be Discerning in Your Rebuke of Others

**A rebuke impresses a man of discernment
more than a hundred lashes a fool (Prov. 17:10).**

This proverb speaks of a wide disparity in forms of discipline. For the wise man, a gentle or mild rebuke is all that's necessary to set matters right. But for a fool, 100 lashes, (more than the number needed to kill him) are needed to create a heart of obedience. In other words, even 100 lashes will not impress a fool.

We are commanded to give reproof to others who offend us (Luke 17: 3), but we are also taught that the effectiveness of that reproof will depend upon the heart of the receiver. In some cases, such as the fool here or the one in Proverbs 27: 22, it will not do any good no matter what form the rebuke takes.

Scriptural Examples

David. David's stony heart became fleshly at the wise rebuke of Nathan in the matter of Bathsheba and Uriah. David confessed his sin before God, and repented (2 Sam. 12:1-7; 13).

Peter. Peter needed only a look from our Lord to break his heart, as he remembered Jesus' prophecy that before the cock crowed, Peter would disown Him three times. It happened just as the Lord had said it would (Luke 22:61-62).

Pharaoh. Time after time the Lord brought disaster upon Pharaoh and the Egyptians and yet the foolish king continually hardened his heart against the Lord's reproof (Ex. 7-15).

Ahaz. This wicked king of Judah was disciplined by God for his foolishness and idol worship. But the rebuke did not humble Ahaz. Rather, it made him more unfaithful (2 Chron. 28:22).

Israel. Isaiah begins his book with a scathing reprimand of Israel. They had been beaten and scourged. Their land was left desolate. God pled with them to come and reason with Him. He offered them forgiveness and healing (Isa. 1).

Prayer of Application

Lord, give me understanding, so that I will be neither too harsh nor too light in the rebuke of others. May I do it in love, that the one reproved would be edified and encouraged.

Find Joy in the Counsel of a Friend

Perfume and incense bring joy to the heart, and the pleasantness of one's friend springs from his earnest counsel (Prov 27:9).

Looking back on my life, one mistake I have made that is predominant over all the rest is that of not always seeking the earnest counsel of godly friends. Of course this one error can lead to countless other troubles and trials, and that is another reason why I would place it at the top of the list.

I fancy myself as an entrepreneur, an innovator, a person who likes to tread ground on which no other has tread before. If I had been born 100 years earlier, I would probably have been a pioneer in a wagon train. Someone once told me that a pioneer is a person with arrows in his backside. Then "pioneer" describes me well, because I've taken lots of arrows there. Some of them went pretty deep and were very painful.

A friend is someone who loves you and wants to see you succeed in life. He earnestly seeks what is best for you. His counsel will therefore be honest and based upon his own experience and education. He may have blind spots, but chances are his blind spots will not be your blind spots. And so he can help you to see the pitfalls that you can't see for yourself.

Scriptural Examples

Mary, her sister Martha, and Jesus. The sisters threw a dinner party for Jesus. Martha served while Mary anointed the Lord's feet with expensive perfume. Here is friendship at its finest. The joy Mary had known as she learned at her Master's feet was now returned by her lavish gift (John 12:1-7).

Peter and Andrew. Peter received joyous counsel from his brother Andrew as the latter ran to find him with the good news that he had found the Messiah. What greater joy can we bring to a friend than to introduce him to the Savior? (John 1: 40,41).

Prayer of Application

O Lord, thank You for the wise counsel of friends and godly men of the church. Help me to humbly submit to sincere rebuke and advice, earnestly seeking it and acting upon it.

My Personal Action Plan

STUDY QUESTIONS

1. Make a list of the difficulties and problems that you have experienced in life. How do you think those trials have helped you to grow as a man and as a child of God? In what practical ways can you draw upon your own difficult experiences to help other men going through the same trials?

2. Here's one for married guys only: How often do you consult the wisdom of your wife for help with your trials and problems? Do you think that her perspective as a woman and as someone who knows you intimately might be of benefit? Turn to Genesis 2:18. What does God mean here by "helper"?

3. In Romans 12:10, Paul commands us to "be devoted to one another in brotherly love. Honor one another above yourselves." How does that verse speak to our need to enter into mentoring relationships? (See Rom. 15:14 for a hint.)

4. In Matthew 15:14, Jesus speaks of the Pharisees as "blind guides." Those who follow them will fall into a pit. Does this mean we are not to accept advice from secular men? Or, should we use it, but consider the source?

PROVERBS TO PONDER
12:15; 15:22; 27:6, 10; 28:23

ONE TO MEMORIZE
The way of a fool seems right to him,
but a wise man listens to advice (Prov. 12:15).

MAKING APPLICATION
My personal action plan to establish mentoring relationships:

1)_____ 2)_____

3)_____ 4)_____

.Chapter *Two*.
A MAN AND HIS MENTORS
···

Part Two:
God's Discipline

Some may find it strange to find a discussion of the discipline of God in a chapter about mentoring or discipling. After all, when we think of mentoring, we think of Christian brothers. But God is part of the mentoring process, too.

While Christian brothers sit down and speak to one another as they engage in mentoring, God works behind the scenes. Yes, He works through His Word, but He also uses what my pastor likes to call the "heat." Every one of us will go through the heat at one time or another in our lives. The heat is to soften us, to make us more pliable, to grow us, and to change us into the likeness of God's Son (Rom. 8:29). By discipline, we are discipled.

God loves us with a love so great that we cannot imagine it. The heat may seem to be a strange way to show His love, but it speaks to the magnitude of our depravity and our need for the holiness that is found only in Him.

Covet Divine Instruction

**Where there is no revelation, the people cast off restraint;
but blessed is he who keeps the law (Prov. 29:18).**

The KJV translates the first line of this verse, "Where there is no vision the people perish." That translation has led many to think it is speaking of a vision for the future. But the proverb's "vision" is really divine revelation, or more precisely, "instruction." The Hebrew word *para* is the word used in Exodus 32:25 when the Israelites "cast off restraint" (see below). This is emphasized by the antithetical parallelism of the second phrase, "but blessed is he who keeps the law."

In 1962, the Ten Commandments were ripped from the walls of our public schools in America, and the skids were greased for America's descent into lawlessness. This act of violence against God's law has had exactly the result predicted by this proverb. Our public schools have disintegrated, and with them the moral and spiritual character of our nation.

The school bulletin board is not the only venue from where God's instruction has been thrown out. In many churches across America, the clear teachings of God have been set aside in favor of "politically correct" human teachings (1 Tim. 4:3). If that happens in your church, you can be sure that your congregation is in decline, as the people begin to cast off restraint.

Scriptural Examples

The Israelites. When Moses returned from the mountain with the first tablets of the Law, he found the people to have "cast off restraint," and to be "running wild." Aaron had succumbed to the demands of the evil crowd and had constructed a golden calf for the people after their own evil hearts (Ex. 32:19-25).

The Israelites. The prophet Hosea spoke of a time when the people of God would be destroyed for lack of knowledge as they reject the divine instruction of God (Hos. 4:1-6).

Prayer of Application

Father, thank You for Your Word, a gracious gift to mankind. We need Your counsel before us on a consistent basis. Without its clear moral instruction, restraints are removed.

Seek a Teachable Spirit

**Whoever loves discipline (instruction) loves knowledge,
but he who hates correction is stupid (Prov. 12:1).**

There is a modern saying to which this proverb speaks: "My mind is already made up; don't confuse me with the facts." Know anyone with a mind like that? The kind of knowledge to which the proverb refers as loved is knowledge of one's own self, and the ultimate knowledge of the state of one's heart.

The natural man thinks of himself as a good guy. Oh, he will admit he's not perfect, but he's "getting better and better every day." But the Bible views man as radically corrupt (Gen. 6:5), and getting worse every day (Titus 3:3). The natural man will shut his ears to this teaching even though the daily newspapers, and his own conscience, scream of its truth.

Only God can show a man the truth about himself. Only God can provide the remedy. Once the need for and the way to a Savior is revealed to us, we should gladly seek the instruction that leads to righteousness. We need to search the Scriptures, for it is there that we look into the mirror that shows us our faults. In His discipline are peace and life everlasting.

Scriptural Examples

Moses/Pharaoh. Moses, on the one hand, was teachable. He originally balked at God's plan to release His people. But from his humility and teachable spirit, God raised up one of the greatest leaders this world has ever known (Ex. 4:10-14).

On the other hand, Pharaoh was thoroughly brutish, hating instruction and not recognizing his own corruption. Time and again God revealed His mighty power to Egypt's king, only to be rebuffed by this foolish man (Ex. 7-14).

Saul (Paul). Saul was unteachable in the true ways of God. But unlike Pharaoh, God chose to circumcise, not harden, Saul's heart. By grace on the Damascus road, he received a new destiny, and a teachable spirit (Acts 9:3-8; 13:9; 26:13-18).

Prayer of Application

Thank You, Lord, for opening my eyes to the awful truth about myself. Help me now to be taught by Your Word, and to obey its instruction, that I might grow in Your love and grace.

Submit to God's Furnace of Purification

**The crucible for silver and the furnace for gold,
but the Lord tests the heart (Prov. 17:3).**

To refine silver and gold, the ore is subjected to tremendous heat, and the precious metal is separated from its impurities. God uses this same principle in people. He does it both to the natural and spiritual man, but for different reasons.

God uses such "heat" to reveal the evil that is in the hearts of those who refuse His grace. He will judge those same hearts in justice by Christ, whom He has raised from the dead (Acts 17:31). God uses the heat to try, but also to refine the heart of the child of God. He melts away our slag of rebelliousness and purifies our hearts to produce the precious fruit He desires. The heat is for our sanctification, to conform us to the image of His Son (Rom. 8:29).

There is no easy way; the child of God must go through the heat. But thank God that there is a purpose for it, that He is producing in us the gold that will last through eternal life.

Scriptural Examples

Abraham. God tested Abraham severely in the matter of offering up for sacrifice his only son, Isaac. Although ultimately God stopped Abraham, God told him that He had given him the trial to test him (Gen. 22:12).

David. David was put through the heat of God's furnace on many occasions. In Psalm 139:23-24, David acknowledged the leadership of God in the testing and purification of his heart.

Hezekiah. When the envoys from Babylon came to Hezekiah, God said He left this king of Judah in order to test him and to see what was in his heart (2 Chron. 32:31).

Jesus. Jesus was tested by Satan, by the Pharisees, by the crushing crowds, and finally by the cross. Even He learned obedience from what He suffered (Heb. 5:7-9).

Prayer of Application

Thank You, Lord, for revealing to me in Your Word that You use the heat in my life for Your eternal purposes: to try my heart, to purify it, and to cause me to bear abundant fruit.

In Discipline, Find the Father's Love

**11) My son, do not despise the Lord's discipline and do not
resent his rebuke, 12) because the Lord disciplines those he
loves, as a father the son he delights in (Prov. 3:11-12).**

I once heard someone say, "Come to Jesus, and all your
problems will be solved." That is very misleading. Nowhere
are we told that we will not have problems on this earth. In fact,
Jesus says, "You will have trouble" (John 16:33). I did not have
earthly trouble until I became a Christian at 33. I wondered,
"Why doesn't God just take me home and spare me from this?"
Since then, I have discovered He keeps us here in part to make
us into the men He wants us to be. We are disciplined for our
good, even as children beloved by the Father (Heb. 12:5-11).

God disciplines those He loves in two ways. One way
begins with our attitude of "I'm going to do my own thing." If
you get away with it, and don't experience God's discipline,
you should tremble, because it's a good bet that you are an
"illegitimate child and not a true son" (Heb. 12:8). If you are
disciplined, take joy in your misery because you are a true son
of God (James 1:2). But there is a better way.

The other way to find the Father's love is by the study and
ingestion of His Word (Ps. 119:11). Scripture is given to us by
God to train us in godliness (2 Tim. 3:16), and to cause us to
grow to maturity in Christ (Heb. 5:14). By either path, God will
get you where He wants you to go; but believe me, the latter is
the much more pleasant route.

Scriptural Examples

The Laodicean church. This lukewarm church was rebuked by Christ for its lack of commitment. He stood at the
door of their hearts and knocked. Those who were Christians
would hear His voice and open the door, receiving His discipline and the joy of His subsequent fellowship (Rev. 3:14-33).

Prayer of Application

Lord, thank You for Your hand of discipline as You have
guided me into Your truth through the years. When I leave the
path, You turn me back to the true way.

Invest in Wisdom

**Listen to advice and accept instruction,
and in the end you will be wise (Prov. 19:20).**

Some years ago, our company established a 401(k) plan, by which savings may be deducted tax free from one's paycheck, and then allowed to grow tax free for retirement. How much retirement income an employee will have down the road depends largely upon how much he has contributed each month and upon how long he has participated.

Wisdom is like that 401(k) plan. If a man begins in his youth to make a daily deposit of godly counsel and instruction, in his latter years he will be filled to overflowing in the wealth of wisdom. However, the man who gets a late start will have trouble catching up. Therefore, it is important that we begin early and make those deposits on a regular basis.

How do we invest in wisdom? We should begin with a daily quiet time before God, praying for wisdom, worshiping and praising Him, and interceding for others. We need to daily read and meditate upon God's Word. Each Sunday should be devoted to God, to hear His Word from the pulpit and from wise Sunday school teachers. Finally, let's put God's wisdom into practice! This is the "solid meat" of the mature Christian (Heb. 5:14).

Scriptural Examples

The scoffers. We meet these mockers in the first chapter of Proverbs. Although wisdom cries out to them, they reject such godly instruction. Those who invest in evil and unrighteousness will reap its fruit in their latter days (Prov. 1:20-33).

The licentious young man. In Proverbs chapter 5, we see another young man who would not obey his teachers or listen to his instructors. He became licentious and went in to the adulterous woman and was trapped. At the end of his life, he had come to utter ruin—his flesh and his body were spent and his life had come to no good end (Prov. 5:7-14).

Prayer of Application

Dear heavenly Father, thank You for putting the desire for godly wisdom in my heart. Help me to store it up daily, that by it I might glorify You in every thought, word, and deed.

Be Crowned with Knowledge

**The simple inherit folly,
but the prudent are crowned with knowledge (Prov. 14:18).**

Just as I inherited my facial features from my mom and dad, I also inherited a propensity toward folly that has been handed down through generations since Adam's sin. This folly is the sin nature that has resulted from that sin (Ps. 51:5). For over 33 years I walked in folly, without understanding. Then God put His knowledge into my heart–the knowledge that the end of such folly is death, but the gift of God is eternal life through Jesus Christ (Rom. 6:23). I was saved.

From that moment, God began to impress upon me a principle of obedience that leads to righteousness (Rom. 6:16). He began to place the knowledge of His Word in me. Then in excruciating heat and screeching of brakes, He turned me from the ways of folly to the ways of wisdom. If you have been saved as an adult, God must wean you from lifelong sinful habits. It is a difficult yet blessed road for many.

This sanctification process is a lifelong journey and I still must live with the old nature in this earthly body (Rom. 7:21-23). But soon, I will be eternally set free of it! Thanks be to God, who is able to rescue us (Rom. 7:24-25) and set our feet on the path leading to crowns of life (Rev. 2:10) and righteousness (2 Tim. 4:8) in the life to come.

Scriptural Examples

Adam and Eve. The first couple coveted the knowledge of good and evil, and rebelled against God in their desire for it. What began as a search for wisdom and knowledge ended in folly and death (Gen. 2:9, 17; 3:6, 22).

Noah. This patriarch refused to be swept along by the folly of the pre-Flood world. In God's knowledge, he built an ark and preached to the simple in their folly, but no one responded. Only Noah and his family were saved (Gen. 6:5-22).

Prayer of Application

Dear Father, what folly it is to walk in my own power, trusting in my own righteousness. Help me to turn from sin to Your knowledge, not in my power, but in that of Your Spirit.

My Personal Action Plan

STUDY QUESTIONS

1. Have you ever gone through the heat – the fire of God's testing? What happened? How did you know it was God at work? How were you changed from the experience? Did God harden or soften others because of it?

2. Read Deuteronomy 4:32-40. How did God discipline the nation Israel in the wilderness in order to make them ready to enter the Promised Land? What events triggered God's discipline? (See Exodus 32 and Numbers 14, for instance.)

3. In Job 5:17, Eliphaz, one of Job's friends, said, "Blessed is the man whom God corrects; so do not despise the discipline of the Almighty." He was right in that statement, but was he right in applying it to Job's situation?

4. In John 15:2 we are told of the heavenly Gardener. What is He doing with His pruning shears? What is the distinction He makes between the branch that He prunes and the one He lops off? What is His purpose?

5. Hebrews 12 is a wonderful chapter regarding God's loving discipline towards us. What are the two benefits spoken of in verse 11? How would you define them?

PROVERBS TO PONDER
6:23; 13:10; 15:10; 15:31-32; 21:11; 28:14

ONE TO MEMORIZE
Whoever loves discipline loves knowledge,
but he who hates correction is stupid (Prov. 12:1).

MAKING APPLICATION
My personal action plan to submit to God's disciplining hand:

1)_____ 2)_____

3)_____ 4)_____

.Chapter *Two*.
A MAN AND HIS MENTORS

Part Three:
A Man's Parents

My parents have been dead for many years. Some of you may never have known your parents. Still others have parents who hate God. Not all of us can take advantage of the mentorship of natural parents. But for most of us, our parents can be a tremendous resource for our growth in the Lord and for the steady fulfillment of our duty as men of God.

But I would also urge every man to think in terms of the larger sense of Exodus 20:12, "Honor your father and your mother...." Elsewhere, Scripture tells us to honor all those in authority over us. That group includes your pastors, your elders, and others in authority. From these men, select a few who can sit down with you from time to time and give you personal counsel. Like your parents, those in authority have responsibility for you and should gladly welcome your request.

Heed Your Parents' Instruction

8) Listen, my son, to your father's instruction and do not forsake your mother's teaching. 9) They will be a garland to grace your head and a chain to adorn your neck (Prov. 1:8-9).

I have a younger sister who lives in Hawaii. One of the great joys of visiting her there is to receive a beautiful, delicate lei. These are chains of aromatic flowers, strung together as garlands to grace the neck of the wearer. This proverb likens our parents' instruction to such fragrant and colorful leis.

The fifth commandment of God, found in Exodus 20:12, is the first that deals with our relationships with other humans. It is the foundational commandment requiring obedience to all those in authority over us, be they in the family, the church (Heb. 13:17), or in the secular government (Rom. 13:1). Those in authority over us are God's earthly representatives to us.

Most of us are grown men and no longer under parental authority. Still, we should not forsake our parents' wise counsel. I grew up in a Christian home, and though my parents are now with the Lord, their teachings still echo in my ears.

What a responsibility we have both as parents and children. As parents, we are to raise our children in the knowledge and admonition of the Lord, and as children, we are to obey the teaching of those who raise us. May God help us and have mercy upon us as we commit this process to Him.

Scriptural Examples

Hophni and Phinehas. These wicked men disgraced their righteous father, Eli, by their ungodliness. They would not listen to their father's rebuke, so God eventually put them both to death (1 Sam. 2:12, 22-24; 4:11).

Adrammelech and Sharezer. These wicked sons of wicked King Sennacherib committed the ultimate sin against their father when they cut him down with the sword (2 Kings 19:37).

Prayer of Application

O Lord, thank You for godly parents who raise their children in Your ways. Help us children to be obedient to their teaching, and to the instruction of all those in authority.

Honor Your Father and Your Mother

**He who robs his father and drives out his mother
is a son who brings shame and disgrace (Prov.19:26).**

This is a picture of corruption in its most radical form. Here is a son who is fed, educated, clothed, and kept in safety throughout his childhood and youth. He is nurtured, loved, and tenderly disciplined by this couple who disregard their own needs and comfort for him. Then, when he is an adult, he steals his father's home and possessions, and evicts his mother, throwing her out on the street to fend for herself.

God commands that we honor our parents (Ex. 20:12). The command was placed before the commandment against murder, and came with a promise. Those who kept it could expect long life in the land God was giving them. What of those who failed to keep it? Proverbs 30: 17 gives us a picture of the punishment one such as this could expect. His eye would be pecked out by the ravens. He would be consumed by the vultures.

Scriptural Examples

Cain. In Genesis 3:15, Adam and Eve were promised that an offspring (seed) of the woman would crush the serpent's head. I believe they thought Cain would be this one, not realizing that the promise would be fulfilled centuries later in Christ, the seed of Mary. What a shame Cain was to his father and mother who had expected so much (Gen. 4:1-16).

Absalom. Absalom's father was David. He rebelled against his father and sought to set himself up as king over Israel (2 Sam.15:1-14). He lay with his father's concubines in the sight of all Israel (2 Sam. 16:20-22). Ultimately, Absalom's death at the hands of David's army caused David tremendous pain and torment. Surely Absalom wasted his father (2 Sam.18:33).

Timothy. Timothy was a man who honored his mother, Eunice, and his grandmother Lois (2 Tim. 1:5).

Prayer of Application

Dear God, thank You for my parents and for their self sacrifice in raising me from infancy. They were not perfect, but they deserve my respect and love. Help me to honor them.

Honor Your Parents and You Honor God
A wise son brings joy to his father,
but a foolish man despises his mother (Prov. 15:20).

The greatest joys in life, and the deepest hurts, are both experienced by parents. What a delight it is to have a son or daughter whose trust is in the Lord and who is prospering in the true way. Conversely, what great pain and unrest lie in the heart of the Christian parent whose child is headstrong and disobedient, and who rejects the Lord's love for him or her.

The unselfish love of a mother is a tiny glimpse for us humans into the heart of God. For truly, God has given us His only Son, the most expensive gift imaginable, that we might have eternal life. So, too, our dear mothers give of themselves without thought of repayment, to give us life and then sustenance on this earth. The child who despises such great love surely deserves the title of "fool."

Scriptural Examples
King David. Much of the trouble David reaped in his sons was due to his own sin against Bathsheba and her husband. In 1 Kings 1:48, however, David rejoices and worships God because his wise son, Solomon, has been placed on the throne.

King David. David wept over the death of his rebellious son Absalom who wanted to be king. Absalom's horrible death shows how seriously God views the parent/child relationship. He will not let the rebellious go unpunished (2 Sam. 18:33).

Mary. The epitome of motherhood, Mary's joy and pain certainly exceeded the boundaries of normal human experience (Luke 2:19; Luke 21:34-35).

Ruth. Witness the love of Ruth for her mother-in-law, Naomi. What joy the widow found in the Moabitess' faithful companionship. And what a reward God had in store for the beautiful Ruth, as she brought Him honor (Ruth 1:16-18).

Prayer of Application
Dear Father, You gave me parents for my great benefit, and I thank You for them. Help me to always honor them, for in doing so I bring honor and glory to You.

Beware of Cursing Those in Authority

If a man curses his father or mother, his lamp will be snuffed out in pitch darkness (Prov. 20:20).

In this proverb, we see a man who is in total violation of the commandment in which God orders us to honor our parents, and indeed, all those in authority over us (Ex. 20:12). It is the first commandment with a promise attached, but the other side of the coin is here. The child who curses his parents will himself be cursed, and will be left in "pitch darkness."

For the Jew, the blessing of God was seen as the light of God. In Numbers 6:22-26, God tells Moses how to bless the Israelites. The Lord's blessing was His face shining upon them. (See also Psalms 4:6; 31:16; 80:3, 7, 19; 104:15; 119:135.) On the cross, God the Father turned His back, as it were, on Jesus, and darkness consumed the land (Matt. 27:45). Darkness, or the absence of light, is a manifestation of separation from God. In Matthew 22:13, Jesus tells of the uninvited wedding guests being thrown into obscure darkness. This is the fate of all those who reject the truth and despise authority (Rom. 2:8).

Scriptural Examples

The Recabites. Jonadab, son of Recab, ordered his sons not to drink wine or build houses or plant vineyards. When Jeremiah set bowls of wine in front of them, they would not drink, saying that they would rather honor the command of their father. God then contrasted their obedience with the disobedience of Israel, who shunned the authority of His Word (Jer. 35:1-14).

Eli's sons. The sons of this man of God were disobedient and a stench to their father's nostrils. They refused to listen to Eli's rebukes, so the Lord put them to death (1 Sam. 2:22-25).

The stubborn son. The parents of the disobedient and rebellious son were to take him to the elders and then to the men of the town, who were to stone him to death (Deut. 21:18-21).

Prayer of Application

Dear Father, how we as humans are so quick to despise authority. Help me, Lord, to honor my parents and all those in authority over me, as all authority has been instituted by You.

Sons: Do Not Grieve Your Parents

**15) My son, if your heart is wise, then my heart will be glad;
16) my inmost being will rejoice
when your lips speak what is right (Prov. 23:15-16).**

The Bible speaks of the heart of man as being the very locus or center of his character. Our Lord testified that out of a man's heart flow all sorts of evil words and deeds (Matt. 15:19-20). Indeed, out of the heart are the very issues of life.

The heart is also the residence of joy (Ps. 4:7) and of deep sorrow (Ps. 13:2). The word "heart" is used 107 times in the Psalms. This shouldn't surprise us, for in the Psalms we find the deep longings, the joys, and the sorrows of a man's heart in his thirst to know God. David, the great king and psalmist, was a man after God's own wise heart (Acts 13:22).

The wise heart is the heart instructed by the wisdom of God. For Christian parents, all other hopes for their children dim in comparison to the hope that their children will be wise in heart. The child of the Christian parent may grow to achieve worldly greatness and to be highly honored among men. But if that child does not obey the One True God, there is a heaviness in the heart of his mother and father. Young man, bring joy to your parents in the wisdom of a heart that loves God.

Scriptural Examples

Paul. In 1 Thessalonians 2:19-20, we see Paul as a father to a church, this time in Thessalonica. Far from his scathing disipline of the Corinthians, he expresses to the Thessalonians that they are his glory and joy. He would glory because of them.

The prodigal son's dad. The prodigal son, who had grieved his father, decided to leave the pigsties and go home. On seeing his son coming from a distance, the father's heart leapt for joy. He ran out to meet the lad and received him back into his household with thanksgiving (Luke 15:13-24).

Prayer of Application

Lord, what a great joy are the children You give to us. But, at the same time, what great heartache comes to parents whose children do not obey You. May I bring joy to my parents.

Bring Joy to Your Mother and Father

A wise son brings joy to his father,
but a foolish son grief to his mother (Prov. 10:1).

There is a sense in which the Bible is a record book of wise and foolish sons who either blessed or cursed their parents. On page after page we find examples of men and women who either brought joy or grief to their mothers and fathers.

Adam, the son of God, grieved his Father. Adam was in turn grieved heavily by Cain, but blessed by both Abel and Seth. The patriarch Abraham was blessed by Isaac, who in turn was grieved by Jacob. The list goes on.

Notice it is the wise son who brings joy and the foolish son who brings grief. Proverbs 1:7 and 9:10 say that wisdom begins with the fear of the Lord. All wisdom flows from that spring. The foolish son, on the other hand, despises the Lord and His instruction. And so it is in our relationship to the Lord that we bring our parents joy. Someone says, "My parents couldn't care less about God. They are upset about my faith in Christ. Have I failed to honor them?" No. You owe more allegiance to your Father in heaven. To bring Him joy is your greater calling.

Scriptural Examples

Noah. We are told in Genesis 5:28-29 that Lamech named his son Noah because Noah would comfort him and his wife in the labor of the soil that God had cursed. Noah did prove to be a wise son who feared the Lord, preached of His righteousness, and followed His instructions to the letter (2 Pet. 2:5; Heb. 11:7).

Ham, Shem, and Japheth. These sons of Noah are the ancestors of all who walk the earth. Following the Flood, Noah foolishly got drunk and lay naked in his tent. Ham disgraced his father by looking at his nakedness and joking about it to the others. But Shem and Japheth backed into the tent and covered their father, thereby honoring him (Gen. 9:21-23).

Prayer of Application

Dear God, comfort and strengthen parents who must suffer in the wake of a son who runs from You. At the same time, help us sons to honor our parents out of love for You.

My Personal Action Plan

STUDY QUESTIONS

1. Do you remember any counsel you received from your parents as a child or young man? What was it? Can you list the topics on a sheet of paper? Did you adopt their counsel and apply it to your life? Do you still do so? What has been the fruit in your life of acceptance or rejection of their counsel?

2. Rehoboam became king of Israel following his father Solomon's death. In 1 Kings 12:1-17 we find the story of his first few days as king. He did not reign over all of Israel for very long. Why? How did he fail? What do you suppose caused him to err? Have you ever done anything like that?

3. In Ruth 3:1-4, Naomi gives counsel to her daughter-in-law. What was the counsel? Did Ruth follow through on it (vv. 5-15)? What was the fruit of Naomi's counsel? What would have been different had Naomi's counsel not been sought?

4. Jesus, in Luke 15:11-24, tells the story of a son who ran away from home with his inheritance. He does not say that the boy's dad counseled him against it, but do you think he did? Would your dad have counseled you against it? Would you counsel your son against going to a far away country? Why?

PROVERBS TO PONDER
4:1-27; 6:20-23; 15:5; 19:13a; 28:24

ONE TO MEMORIZE
A wise man brings joy to his father,
but a foolish man despises his mother (Prov. 15:20).

MAKING APPLICATION
My personal action plan to seek counsel of those in authority:

1)_____ 2)_____

3)_____ 4)_____

.Chapter Three.
A MAN AND
HIS INTEGRITY

Our heavenly Father is a God of ultimate integrity. Put simply, that means you and I can believe what He says, trusting Him to fulfill His every promise. God's righteous character is displayed perfectly in what He does and He wants you and me to mirror His character in every facet of our lives.

When God brought His chosen people out of bondage in Egypt, He said to them, "Therefore be holy, because I am holy" (Lev. 11:45). As Christians, we too have this call to holiness and good works (Eph. 2:10). The call extends into every area of our spiritual, moral, and sexual lives. Indeed, His holiness should be reflected in every thought we allow in our minds, and in every word that passes from our lips.

In this chapter, we will see what wisdom the Proverbs have for us as we seek to live lives that please the One who has brought us out of sin's bondage.

.Chapter Three.
A MAN AND HIS INTEGRITY

· ·

Part One:
Spiritual Purity

Spiritual sins are those at the very center of one's being. For instance, I believe the Bible teaches that the underlying sin of all mankind is a world view which excludes the Living and True God. Psalm 10:4 says, "In his pride the wicked does not seek him; in all his thoughts there is no room for God." All of the wicked man's sins flow from that one false principle in his heart, the seat of his being. It is the sin of unbelief.

Spiritual pride, of which the psalmist speaks, obscures the truth that would set man free to seek God. But if one word could be found to describe fallen man, I would submit the word, "Idolater." Idolatry seeks to set up gods in place of the True God. They are "man-made gods [that] are no gods at all" (Acts 19:26). We who have been justified by faith in Christ need to beware of these sins, as well as those of spiritual slothfulness and inconsistency that can detract from the purity to which our God has called us.

Walk the Straight Path of Integrity

**The man of integrity walks securely,
but he who takes crooked paths will be found out (Prov. 10:9).**

My dictionary defines "integrity" as "soundness of moral character; a sound, unimpaired condition, or wholeness and completeness." A man of integrity is one who has adopted certain moral principles in life, and then walks according to them. For the man of God, the Bible forms the basis of those principles. The Bible is the Christian's only authority for faith and life. Only the Bible can bind his conscience. Therefore, if the Christian is to walk in integrity, he must walk in conformity to God's Word. To do so is to walk securely, without fear of failure or shame.

How do we obey this proverb's principle and keep on the path of integrity? The bad news is that we can't. However, the good news is that the Spirit of God working in our hearts by faith can! We can do all things through Him (Phil. 4:13).

Scriptural Examples

Enoch and the antidiluvians. Enoch walked so closely in integrity with his God that God took him home. He never tasted death. All the while, he lived among men who walked in crooked paths (Gen. 5:22-24; 6:5; Heb. 11:5).

Job. God commended Job as a man who feared God and walked in integrity. Job would be the first to tell us that his integrity came only from his God (Job 1:8; 2:3; 2:9; 6:29; 27:5).

Hanani. Nehemiah put this man in charge of Jerusalem because he was a man of integrity and feared God (Neh. 7:2).

Peter. Peter was one who got off the path. Paul found out and rebuked Peter because he had left the true gospel in order to appease the Judaizers (Gal. 2:11-14).

Ananias and Sapphira. This couple was on a crooked path. God took them home, but not like Enoch (Acts 5:1-10).

Prayer of Application

Sovereign Lord, thank You for Your Word and for the Holy Spirit who helps me to follow the Word's secure path. May I always walk in its light, to the end that You will be glorified in me.

Flee from Spiritual Sloth

13) The sluggard says, "There is a lion in the road, a fierce lion roaming the streets!" 14) As a door turns on its hinges, so a sluggard turns on his bed. 15) The sluggard buries his hand in the dish; he is too lazy to bring it back to his mouth. 16) The sluggard is wiser in his own eyes than seven men who answer discreetly (Prov. 26:13-16).

The sluggard of Proverbs is faithless (13), feckless (14), foodless (15), and foolish (16). He neglects his responsibilities to his family, work, and friends, and you can be certain that he will neglect his larger spiritual duty to God. Let's see how these verses describe the spiritual sluggard.

First, in verse 13, he is spiritually *faithless*. He will not step out on faith to do anything. He always has an excuse. There may not really be "a lion in the road," but something is always standing between the sluggard and his duty.

Second, in verse 14, he is spiritually *feckless*, or irresponsible. A door never leaves the door jamb. Neither is the sluggard's life going anywhere. He is without goals or the strategies for attaining those goals. He likes his soft bed, but can doze just as easily in a pew on Sunday morning.

Third, in verse 15, the sluggard is spiritually *foodless*. While he may know some Christian jargon, the deep things of Christ are avoided. He is a spiritual baby, feeding on baby food and milk, not able to chew on the real meat of the Word (Heb. 5:13, 14). Why? Because a deeper knowledge of God may convict him of his sloth and awaken him from his slumber.

Finally, in verse 16, the spiritual sluggard is *foolish*. He is puffed up in pride. He bluffs his way through life, not understanding that his superficiality is as plain to others as the nose on his face. Do not join the spiritual sloth. Rather, flee from sloth, and join with those who in humility and diligence work out their salvation with fear and trembling (Phil. 2:12).

Prayer of Application

Father, keep me from spiritual sloth. I know how easy it is to forsake Bible study, prayer, and reflection, and instead seek my own pleasure. Help me to live faithfully before You.

Flee from the Barrenness of Idolatry
**Like clouds and wind without rain is a man
who boasts of gifts he does not give (Prov. 25:14).**

Proverbs 25:13 speaks of the refreshment given to men by the faithful messenger. Here is the unfaithful messenger, a man who promises gifts, but never delivers. Rain that would refresh the earth and bring forth fruit never comes. Here is a covetous rich man who announces that he is going to give a big gift to the church, but somehow the money never arrives. He may be the man who promises to enter an agreement, but never goes through with the deal. (Sound familiar, you salesmen?)

But I believe that there is a wider application here: idolatry. Both you and I are idolators because of the sin that is in our hearts. Given the chance, we will run to the first promise that looks good, forsaking the promises of God. And when we place our hope in anything over and above the promises and providence of God, we are into idolatry. And exactly what is the idol to which we will run? It is someone or something which boasts of gifts that he or it does not give.

God is the One who brings all good gifts. There is no other ultimate giver (James 1:17). He gives us new life and sends the rain to refresh us and to cause our fruit to grow. Hope in God and God alone for every good and perfect gift.

Scriptural Examples
Satan. This deceiver boasted of gifts he did not give as he misled the first couple. Instead, he brought death (Gen. 3:3-5).

Idols. The Israelites often worshipped the gods of the other nations. But these "gods" were nothing but wood and stone. Men like idols because idols put no demands upon them.

False teachers. Both Peter and Jude speak of these men as "clouds without rain" and "springs without water." How different they are from our faithful pastors (Jude 11-13; 2 Pet. 2:17).

Prayer of Application
Lord, keep me from idolatry. I become enamored easily with the ways of this world. Help me to put all my confidence in You, Lord, as the source of every good and perfect gift.

Beware of Pride that Goes Before a Fall

**Before his downfall a man's heart is proud,
but humility comes before honor (Prov. 18:12).**

I lived through the truth of this verse. When I was saved in 1971, I was with a large commercial real estate brokerage firm. In 1972, I decided to leave that organization and start my own development company. God had been "real smart" to save me, and I was going to "cut a wide swath" for Him, making lots of money for His kingdom. My real motives, of course, were to pridefully create a name for myself and to live a life of luxury.

Three years later, I owed more money than I ever could hope to repay. I moved my family to Florida in order to earn a living. There, for the next six years, God continued to humble me. Returning to San Diego, I started a business in 1981 with only an idea and virtually no money. God has prospered that company, and has allowed me to pay my development debts.

No longer does honor from men appeal to me. I have learned much in the school of God's discipline, the most important lesson being that one should live his life for God alone. If the Lord God wants to honor me, that's His business. My business is to humbly obey Him.

Scriptural Examples

Uzziah. This king of Judah became very prideful. He entered the temple to burn incense to the Lord, an activity only allowed the priests, and God struck him with leprosy. He carried that disease until the day he died (2 Chron. 26:16-21).

Satan. Described in these verses as the "king of Tyre," Satan is said to have become proud of his beauty, and so his wisdom was corrupted. God threw him out of heaven (Ezek. 28:17).

Moses. We are told here that Moses was a very humble man, more so than any man who was on the earth. God lifted him up in high honor because of his meekness (Num. 12:3).

Prayer of Application

Heavenly Father, search my heart for the pride that it holds and remove it from me. Place in me a humble spirit that I might only boast in You and of Your grace and providence.

Flee from Spiritual Prostitution

24) Now then, my sons, listen to me; pay attention to what I say. 25) Do not let your heart turn to her ways or stray into her paths. 26) Many are the victims she has brought down; her slain are a mighty throng (Prov. 7:24-27).

Proverbs has much to say about physical adultery, but spiritual adultery is much more serious. In fact, God uses physical adultery as a metaphor for its spiritual counterpart, the false gospel (Hos. 1, 2). These are not really gospels at all, but lies that lead to death (Gal. 1:7).

Like prostitutes hanging from their doorways in any "red light" district, spiritual prostitutes visit doorsteps with their false doctrines, seeking to lead people away from the Savior. They preach a different Christ than the One of Scripture (Luke 21:8), and would lure the unwary with lies and half-truths that can sound good to the spiritually gullible. Beware – don't let your heart turn to their teaching.

Recently, a cult that is growing rapidly throughout the world built a multi-million dollar "temple" nearby. It is beautiful in its stark whiteness against the blue sky, and its presence has lured many thousands to hear the cult's false teaching. That temple is a concrete prostitute, standing at the side of the interstate highway, seeking whom she may devour (1 Pet. 5:8). Avoid the spiritual prostitute. All her paths lead down to the chambers of death.

Scriptural Examples

Gideon. This man was chosen by God to be Israel's judge. He was used to lead a tiny force to victory against a huge army of Midianites. In spite of seeing the power of God at work in this victory, and in his life, Gideon turned to spiritual adultery. He made a golden idol, and Israel then prostituted itself by worshipping the idol in Gideon's hometown (Judg. 8:22-28).

Prayer of Application

Father, thank You for teaching me Your truth through the Word. But many in our land are teaching falsehoods about You, I pray that You would protect the unwary from them.

Look into the Mirror of God's "Hate List"

16) There are six things the Lord hates, seven that are detestable to him: 17) haughty eyes, a lying tongue, hands that shed innocent blood, 18) a heart that devises wicked schemes, feet that are quick to rush into evil, 19) a false witness who pours out lies and a man who stirs up dissension among brothers (Prov. 6:16-19).

Although the number seven usually means completeness, this list is far from a complete list of sins. It is merely representative of some of the sins we commit. Like the FBI's ten most wanted criminals, this list may be God's seven most hated sins.

Notice that God uses members of the body to describe these sins: eyes, tongue, hands, heart, and feet. The list is headed by the sin of pride. God hates the proud look whose bearer thinks too highly of self and too lowly of others and of Him. Pride is the main sin that estranges man from his Creator (Job 20:4-8; Ps. 10:4). Because of pride, people don't see a need for Christ.

Next, we see a lying tongue, then murder. We are reminded of the innocent blood of millions of little children who have been aborted throughout America and the world. The list continues with scheming hearts, and evil feet which put the evil scheme into shoe leather. Finally, perjurers and men who stir up dissension among brothers are added to this hall of infamy. How do you look in the mirror of God's "hate list"?

Scriptural Examples

The Nicolaitans. In the letter to the church at Ephesus, Jesus stated that He hated the practices of these men. Who were they? Little is known, but they are mentioned in Revelation 2: 14-15 in the context of the Balaamites who were idolators and sexually immoral people in Moses' day. They may have been a pseudo-Christian sect that expressed its freedom in libertine behavior or gnostics who worshipped the emperor (Rev. 2:6).

Prayer of Application

Search me Lord and know my heart, test me and know my anxious thoughts. See if there is any offensive way in me and lead me in the way everlasting. Keep me on the right path.

My Personal Action Plan

STUDY QUESTIONS

1. Read Psalm 25. In what (or in whom) does the psalmist's hope lie? Will integrity and uprightness necessarily protect us in this life? In what way? If it will not, will it ever? What are you hoping for? In what or in whom are you hoping?

2. In Acts 20:22-25, Paul bids farewell to his friends in Ephesus. Did he expect protection from hardships on his journey? Like the sluggard in Proverbs 26:13, Paul saw a "lion in the road." What was his reaction to it? Look now at 2 Timothy 4:17. What is Paul's testimony?

3. In Colossians 3:5, Paul says that greed is idolatry. Why do you think that this is true? Is it now, or has it ever been, true in your life? Can the other sins he lists be idols also?

4. In Deuteronomy 8, Moses speaks to the Israelites about their walk with God. Why did God lead them in the desert for 40 years? What was God's top priority for them? What concerns did Moses have for the people in the Promised Land? Were Moses' concerns fulfilled in their history there? Did God's threat of verses 19 and 20 ever have to be carried out?

PROVERBS TO PONDER
4:3-7; 4:26; 11:23; 15:19; 19:23-24

ONE TO MEMORIZE
Before his downfall a man's heart is proud,
but humility comes before honor (Prov. 18:12).

MAKING APPLICATION
My personal action plan to maintain spiritual purity:

1)_____ 2)_____

3)_____ 4)_____

.Chapter Three.
A MAN AND HIS INTEGRITY

Part Two:
Moral Purity

While spiritual purity speaks of our direct walk and relationship with God, moral purity speaks to our walk in this world. Yet the two are closely related. Moral impurity affects the spiritual and vice versa.

In Part Two of "A Man and His Integrity," we will examine a few aspects of what it means to be morally pure. Others will be covered in Parts Three and Four ahead. Here, we will look at purity in our thought life, honesty in dealing with our fellowman, self-control, overindulgence in food and alcoholic beverages, and our capacity for rationalization, or that innate ability we humans have to pardon ourselves for immoral behavior by assigning it a fictitious cause.

Walk the High Road of Moral Purity

**He whose walk is blameless is kept safe, but he
whose ways are perverse will suddenly fall (Prov. 28:18).**

While we may want to see believers in line one of this proverb, and unbelievers in line two, I want to apply it just to believers. One Christian steers a course of integrity, and the other a course of compromise. They both may be heading for heaven, but one is on the high road and the other on the low.

The higher path is not necessarily the easier path. Believers are called to suffer pain in this world and oftentimes the most blameless suffers the most (Job 1:1). But God draws a great distinction between different reasons for suffering (1 Pet. 2:20-21). Suffering for righteousness' sake is praiseworthy, but suffering for sin is not. Let's look at two biblical examples of men who took opposite paths.

Scriptural Examples

Two prophets: Daniel and Jonah. Both of these men were called to serve God outside of the nation Israel–Daniel in Babylon, and Jonah in Nineveh. Daniel served with integrity, and even though he suffered, God carried him through it to safety. Jonah, on the other hand, refused God's orders. He was thrown from the ship for his sin and only by God's grace rescued by a giant fish. God brought Jonah through his trials also, but was not pleased with his ways.

Two patriarchs: Abraham and Lot. Both of these men trusted God for salvation (2 Pet. 2:7). But Lot went down to wicked Sodom with his family, while Abraham stayed in the hills. The destruction of Sodom broke Lot's family apart. On the other hand, God never has one word of rebuke for the righteous Abraham. He trusted God and His promises, and although he saw his share of trouble, he became the ancestor of all who would receive God's free gift of salvation (Gen. 12-15, 19).

Prayer of Application

Dear heavenly Father, keep my feet on the high path of Your law, Lord, for I am powerless to follow it unless Your Spirit provides strength and stability for my daily walk.

Let Purity Dominate Your Thought Life

**Death and Destruction lie open before the Lord –
how much more the hearts of men! (Prov. 15:11).**

There is no place in all of creation that is not open and visible to our omniscient, omnipresent God. He sees into the hearts and minds of every man and woman. The natural man scoffs at such a notion, and goes on thinking sinful thoughts.

In contrast, the child of God understands that God has access to his thoughts. He seeks to allow God to control his thoughts (Gal. 5:16-18), for he knows that thoughts precede actions. The impurities that remain remind the Christian of his sinfulness and urge him toward closer fellowship with Christ.

How do you allow God to control your mind? One way may be to think of your mind as a blackboard. Ask God to write on it only thoughts that are pleasing to Him. What thoughts are pleasing to God? Whatsoever is true, noble, right, pure, lovely, admirable, excellent, or praiseworthy, think on such things, and the God of peace will be with you (Phil. 4:8-9).

Scriptural Examples

Aaron. His rebellious thoughts were known to God as surely as were Moses' angry words and swift rod at the waters of Meribah (Num. 20:12, 24).

The Jews. Jehovah said that He would punish the Hebrews who even thought that He would not act (Zeph. 1:12).

The Pharisees. Jesus knew the evil thoughts these adversaries harbored in their minds. He read their minds like a book, and often answered them before they spoke (Luke 5:22).

Nebuchadnezzar. This Babylonian king wanted his wise men to not only interpret his dream, but to tell him exactly what the dream was. God gave Daniel the dream that the king would not tell anyone, thereby allowing Daniel to witness to the omniscience of Almighty God (Dan. 2:29).

Prayer of Application

Dear Lord, purify my thoughts. May every one of them come into subjection to Your will. Search my mind, O Lord, see if there are any wicked thoughts there, and purify me.

Practice Absolute Honesty

**Differing weights and differing measures –
the Lord detests them both (Prov. 20:10).**

If a man owns a grocery store and permits its produce scales
to weigh just a slight bit heavy, so that for every true pound of
potatoes he is charging for 1.02 pounds, then he has stolen from
his customer just as certainly as if he had pilfered the stereo
from his customer's car. Actually, what the groceryman has
done may be worse than common burglary, because he has
done it in the context of a seemingly honest business transac-
tion in which an innocent party is tricked.

We Christians must practice squeaky clean honesty in all
our dealings. We must do this not just because we know that
our God is omniscient and that His judgment is like a consum-
ing fire (Heb. 12:29). But we are to do it primarily out of love for
Christ and a desire to see His name glorified in us.

Scriptural Examples

Satan. Called "the king of Tyre," it is nevertheless Satan
who is described by Ezekiel. At one time a blameless and
beautiful creature, Satan's heart became proud and he engaged
in sins and dishonest trade. Satan is the father of lies (John 8:44)
and the father of dishonest scales, too (Ezek. 28:12-19).

Jacob. Although Jacob used dishonest means to steal his
brother Esau's birthright and in some of his dealings with his
father-in-law Laban, toward his latter years God changed him.
When his sons returned from Egypt, Jacob insisted that they
return the silver in their sacks (Gen. 43:12).

Judas. Judas complained to Jesus that the perfume lav-
ished upon Him by Martha's sister Mary was a waste. He said
its value could have been given to the poor. But Judas did not
care about the poor. He was a dishonest schemer who would
probably have kept the money for himself (John 12:4-6).

Prayer of Application

Lord, every day I run into situations where my honesty is
tested. It may be in financial matters, in my associations, or in
my home. Help me, Lord, to be honest in every way.

Practice Self-Control

**Like a city whose walls are broken down
is a man who lacks self-control (Prov. 25:28).**

In the ancient world and through the Middle Ages, cities were fortified with walls against the potential attack of invading armies. Sometimes, other barriers such as moats and pits were also constructed, but the walls of a city were its ultimate protection. A breach in the city's walls during a battle meant disaster, as the invaders poured into the city.

We too have walls like those ancient cities and enemies who seek to break through the weak spots and destroy us. How do we keep our walls from being breached? First, let's admit our weaknesses. Do a complete self-inventory just as Nehemiah inventoried the walls of Jerusalem that had been broken down (Neh. 2:3-5). Second, humbly submit to God's Spirit in prayer, asking for strength to reinforce those weaknesses (Matt. 26:41). Third, share your weaknesses with close friends, asking them for prayer and support. There is strength and encouragement in numbers, particularly in times of temptation.

What are the results of the breach of a personal wall? A witness for Christ is limited or destroyed. A life of service is hobbled or even shut down. The joy of purity is extinguished in guilt and sadness. Families are broken apart. There is loss of heavenly reward (1 Cor. 9:27). Watch your walls with care and prayer. A breach in the walls can be devastating.

Scriptural Examples

Paul. Paul boasted of his weaknesses. Why? Because he realized that it was through his weakness that the Lord's strength could be manifested. When he complained to God about a certain thorn in his flesh, the Lord said, "My grace is sufficient for you, for my power is made perfect in weakness." This same power is available to each of us (2 Cor. 12:7-10).

Prayer of Application

Father, thank You for the power to live my life in a way that is pleasing to You. But I have weaknesses in my walls that need constant attention. Help me to be strong in You.

Do Not Cross the Line of Intemperance

19) Listen, my son, and be wise, and keep your heart on the right path. 20) Do not join those who drink too much wine or gorge themselves on meat, 21) for drunkards and gluttons become poor, and drowsiness clothes them in rags (Prov. 23:19-21).

Driving home the other day, I saw three men dressed in rags. As I drove by, one of the men raised a quart of beer to his lips and took a big swig. Sadly, it was a perfect picture of this proverb's message to us. Even sadder is the fact that this scene is repeated many thousands of times across our country today.

I believe that Scripture teaches beneficial aspects of alcoholic beverages (1 Tim. 5:23), used as intended and in moderation (Titus 1:7). Certainly meat, or food, is a necessity of life. We would starve to death if we did not eat. But to cross the line into drunkenness and gluttony by letting a substance control our thoughts and actions is expressly forbidden by Scripture.

George Lawson says it like this: "Although we do not dethrone reason by drinking, yet if we impair the vigor of it, and render ourselves less fit for the business of life, and the service of God, than we are at other times, by the free use of the bottle, we are wine-bibbers" (p.407). In other words, if our use of alcohol or food ever leaves us feeling less fit for the service of men and of God, then it has become our master.

Scriptural Examples

The Corinthians. Some of the converts to the faith in Corinth were overindulging in food and wine at church dinners. Others in their midst had nothing to eat or drink (1 Cor. 11:20-22).

Jesus. His enemies called our Lord a wine-bibber and a glutton. They had earlier criticized John the Baptist, who "came neither eating nor drinking," of having a demon. While Jesus was a friend of sinners, like those homeless men in the illustration above, He was never guilty of this, or any, sin (John 2:1-11).

Prayer of Application

Father, there are many things in this life that can become my master if I let my guard down. Help me in all ways to keep my eyes fixed on You and fit for service in Your kingdom.

Beware of Your Ability to Rationalize

**The Lord detests differing weights,
and dishonest scales do not please him (Prov. 20:23).**

Whenever a verse is repeated, we need to grasp the seriousness of its warning. This proverb's rebuke is heard four times in the book, twice in chapter 20 itself (Prov. 11:1; 16:11; and 20:10). God detests deceit with a capital "D."

As heirs of the sin nature, we can deceive not only one another, but ourselves as well. Much of our self-deceit lies in our capacity to rationalize, or to ascribe fictitious causes to our moral choices. Flip Wilson cried, "The devil made me do it!" We need to be suspicious of all our motives, filtering everything through the grid of God's Word, and praying that the Holy Spirit will keep us away from the abomination of deceit.

The work of the Holy Spirit at regeneration put a desire in my heart to do what is pleasing in God's sight. But only through the Spirit of God working in my heart and mind, moment by moment, can I be empowered to do it, and overcome the deceit that still lurks within me (Rom. 7:15-25).

Scriptural Examples

Shelemiah, Zadok, Pedaiah, and Hanan. These men were said by Nehemiah to be trustworthy and were placed in charge of distributing supplies to their brothers (Neh. 13:13).

Elymas. This man, whose name meant "sorcerer," opposed Paul and Barnabas at Paphos. The apostle called him an enemy of that which is right, full of deceit and treachery. Paul then proceeded to render Elymas blind for a season, a condition that matched his lack of spiritual sight (Acts 13:6-11).

The Jews. Paul described in Romans 10:2-3 what might be called "The Great Deceit." The Jews, like all people who do not know of the righteousness that comes from God, sought to establish their own, listening to the deceitfulness of their hearts.

Prayer of Application

Gracious God, You have called me to walk honestly in this world. Protect me from my own deceitful heart, which is able to rationalize and excuse in me that which is morally wrong.

My Personal Action Plan

STUDY QUESTIONS

1. In 1 John 3:18-22, we are cautioned not to love with words and the tongue but with actions and in truth. What is the difference? What are the benefits in doing this for our assurance? Our peace? Our confidence? Our prayers?

2. In Amos 8:1-7, God is furious with the people of Israel. What business practices had they set up that caused God such anger? In what did the businessmen hope? How do you know?

3. In the first eleven verses of his second general epistle, Peter encourages moral purity for all who know Christ. What does he say in 1:3 that we lack for purity and godliness? What seven moral attributes are we to add to our faith? For what five reasons are we to make every effort to add them?

4. Turn to Exodus 1:15-19. The king of Egypt ordered Shiphrah and Puah to kill the Hebrew male children. They refused. What principle, if any, can we draw from their refusal?

5. In the Flood, God destroyed the world. What insight can we glean from Genesis 6:5 as to why He did it? What does this verse say about God's omniscience?

PROVERBS TO PONDER
16:32; 20:1; 23:17-18; 24:15-16; 28:6; 29:1

ONE TO MEMORIZE
Like a city whose walls are broken down
is a man who lacks self-control (Prov. 25:28).

MAKING APPLICATION
My personal action plan to walk in moral purity:

1)_____ 2)_____

3)_____ 4)_____

.Chapter Three.
A MAN AND HIS INTEGRITY

Part Three:
Sexual Purity

Perhaps the greatest temptation we men face in this life is that which would lead us away from sexual purity. I thought age would decrease my sex drive and my propensity to be lured by sexual sin. As I approach 60, it has not happened yet.

In our discussion of sexual purity, we will look again at purity in our thought lives, God's omniscience, and the similarity between physical adultery and its spiritual counterpart. We will also see how much God hates sexual activity outside the marriage covenant. Many people laugh at situation comedies on TV that flaunt adulterous situations. But for God, adultery is no laughing matter.

Avoid Fornication Like the Plague

1) My son, pay attention to my wisdom, listen well to my words of insight, 2) that you may maintain discretion and your lips may preserve knowledge. 3) For the lips of an adulteress drip honey, and her speech is smoother than oil; 4) but in the end she is bitter as gall, sharp as a double-edged sword. 5) Her feet go down to death; her steps lead straight to the grave. 6) She gives no thought to the way of life; her paths are crooked, but she knows it not. 7) Now then, my sons, listen to me; do not turn aside from what I say. 8) Keep to a path far from her, do not go near the door of her house, 9) lest you give your best strength to others and your years to one who is cruel, 10) lest strangers feast on your wealth and your toil enrich another man's house. 11) At the end of your life you will groan, when your flesh and body are spent. 12) You will say, "How I hated discipline! How my heart spurned correction! 13) I would not obey my teachers or listen to my instructors. 14) I have come to the brink of utter ruin in the midst of the whole assembly" (Prov. 5:1-14).

These fourteen verses really need no comment. They may be understood by anyone of maturity, and particularly if one has committed adultery in the past. But there are some interesting features. Notice first the contrast here between the lips of knowledge that protect us (v. 2), and the lips of the adulteress that ooze honey (v. 3). Although her lips promise sweetness and her voice is smoother than oil, in the end she is bitter as gall. All sin is like this. It looks good, feels good, tastes good, and sounds good, so it must *be* good. Right? Wrong!

Extramarital sex, including homosexuality, is destroying the American family. If left unchecked it will destroy our entire society. Abortion, incest, disease, child abuse, divorce, and suicide are all manifestations of the bitter gall being spread by this pleasure-promising sin. Christian, avoid it like the plague that it is.

Prayer of Application

Sovereign Lord, enable me to see the awful consequences of extramarital sex and avoid it at all costs. Let me not even think about sex outside the context of marriage.

Remember, Your God Sees Everything

20) Why be captivated, my son, by an adulteress?
Why embrace the bosom of another man's wife? 21) For a
man's ways are in full view of the Lord, and he examines all
his paths. 22) The evil deeds of a wicked man ensnare him;
the cords of his sin hold him fast. 23) He will die for lack of
discipline, led astray by his own great folly (Prov. 5:20-23).

A man was trying to seduce a woman. He said, "Come on,
who's going to know?" She replied, "There are three who will
know: You will know, I will know, and God will know."

Few people are foolish enough to be atheists. Creation
gives us ample reason to suspect and to even posit a Creator.
But many, including some who call themselves "Christian,"
live as if there is no God (Ps. 14:1-3). These "practical atheists"
think God is in a deep coma. If they would just open the Bible,
they would see the great error in their thinking.

There is another principle here: we are snared by our own
evil deeds (v. 22). An innocent fib becomes a lifelong habit of
lying. A snort of cocaine at a party begins an addiction to drugs.
A sexual encounter at a young age may bring on a guilty
conscience, but the next time it happens there is less guilt. Each
time the sin is repeated the conscience is seared with a thicker
and thicker scar, and finally is hardened to the sin. Repetition
of any practice forms a habit, and the habit becomes our master,
or the cords that hold us fast.

Scriptural Examples

Jesus. On several occasions, Jesus read the very thoughts
of the Pharisees and others. His omniscience was a clear indi-
cation of His deity, for no mere man can see into the mind of
another. When we confess our sins to God, even those of the
heart, we aren't telling Him anything He doesn't already know
(Matt. 12:25; Mark 2:8; Luke 5:22; 6:8; 11:17).

Prayer of Application

Father, I want to make every thought and deed captive to
Your Word. I am comforted by Your omniscience as You are
holding me in the palm of Your hand. Thank You, Lord.

Beware the Deep Pit of God's Wrath

**The mouth of an adulteress is a deep pit;
he who is under the Lord's wrath will fall into it (Prov. 22:14).**

One of the most popular TV shows of the 80's and early 90's was the sitcom "Cheers." The series took place in a basement bar in Boston whose denizens included a bartender/owner named Sam Malone. Sam was a former Red Sox pitcher who was more famous for his exploits in bed than for those on the mound. In many respects, Sam's promiscuity represented the ethos of our culture: "Sex is fun. It feels good so it must be good. Get sex whenever and wherever you can."

But the warning of this proverb is anything but funny. All who succumb to the mouth of the adulteress are under the wrath of an angry God. God gave mankind the gift of sexual intercourse to be enjoyed only in the context of the heterosexual marriage union (Gen. 2:20-25; Heb. 13:4). What a testimony it is to man's depravity that this greatest of life's physical pleasures should be used to mock the Creator who gave it.

The bottom line is this: all sin is insanity. Called to choose heaven, man chooses hell. Only by the grace of God available in the work of the Savior can anyone be saved. But God's love for sinners is deeper than the deepest pit leading to hell. There is no sin so grievous as to restrict God's mercy. God's call is to repent from it and believe in the One who can fully save (1 Tim. 1:16; Isa. 45:22; Acts 2:21).

Scriptural Examples

The Corinthian adulterer. The believers in Corinth had a man in their assembly who was sleeping with his stepmother. And they were proud of it! I am sure that they were like the many Christians today who laugh at shows like "Cheers," but fail to see God's wrath overriding any humor in adultery. Paul told the Corinthians to expel the sinner from their midst (1 Cor. 5:1-3).

Prayer of Application

Father, thank You for the gift of sexuality. Lord, people have perverted Your gift and cheapened it in sin. Help America to forsake the insanity of sexual sin and turn to You for grace.

Don't Even Think About Sexual Sin

**25) Do not lust in your heart after her beauty or let her
captivate you with her eyes, 26) for the prostitute
reduces you to a loaf of bread, and the adulteress
preys upon your very life. 27) Can a man scoop fire into
his lap without his clothes being burned? 28) Can a man
walk on hot coals without his feet being scorched?
29) So is he who sleeps with another man's wife;
no one who touches her will go unpunished (Prov. 6:25-29).**

In the businessmen's Bible study that I lead, we once
embarked on a topical study of the commandments of Christ.
One of our first topics was "Thought Life." The first discussion
was of our Lord's command in Matthew 5:27-28. Like verse 25
in the passage above, He said that even to lust after a woman
was tantamount to adultery. The command hits us men right
between the eyes. But outward sin always begins in the mind.
That is why Proverbs 4:23 insists we guard our hearts.

Scriptural Examples

David. It was a warm evening in Jerusalem. King David got
up from his throne and took the stairs to the roof of his palace in
search of a cooling breeze. He looked down from the tall building and saw on a nearby rooftop a beautiful woman bathing in
the afterglow of the hot day. The vision of her body aroused a
desire in him to have her. Undisturbed that she was the wife of
one of his army commanders now out fighting in the field, David
gave into the passion that stirred within him and caused him to
send for her. Obedient to her king, Bathsheba went to him.

Even though David would later confess his sin and receive
forgiveness, it haunted him the rest of his days. His sinful
thoughts had turned to action and brought an avalanche of
burning coals into his life. Solomon, who penned these verses
in Proverbs, knew this story well. The participants were his
mom and dad (2 Sam. 11:2-4; Ps. 51).

Prayer of Application

Heavenly Father, may the meditations of my heart always
be acceptable in Your sight. May I honor You not only with my
words and deeds, but with my every thought.

Flee from Both Kinds of Adultery

16) [Wisdom] will save you also from the adulteress, from the wayward wife with her seductive words, 17) who has left the partner of her youth and ignored the covenant she made before God. 18) For her house leads down to death and her paths to the spirits of the dead. 19) None who go to her return or attain the paths of life (Prov. 2:16-19).

As we have seen, there are two kinds of adultery, the physical and the spiritual. In Jeremiah 3:8-10, God speaks of adulterous Israel defiling the land with gods of wood and stone. Idolatry is spiritual adultery (Ezek. 23:37), the worship of something created rather than the Creator (Rom. 1:25).

We live in a generation where adultery of both kinds is commonplace. Spiritual adultery today is manifested largely in two ways. First, there is an overarching love for the material things of the world, its pleasures, comforts, riches, and power (James 4:3-5). Love of the things of the world is diametrically opposed to the love of the Father.

The other manifestation of spiritual adultery is in the "smorgasbord" approach to knowing God. Many people do not want to hear sound doctrine, but will hire teachers who will make them comfortable (2 Tim. 4:3). It's as if they were in front of a salad bar: "I'll take some love, but I'll pass on the wrath. Mercy is nice, but I don't want any holiness." But we either take God as He is in His Word, or we do not take Him at all.

Scriptural Examples

Joseph and Potiphar's wife. Today, we might call Joseph a "hunk." He was well built and handsome, we are told, and far removed from family and friends. He was sold to a wealthy Egyptian named Potiphar who put Joseph in charge of his entire household. But Potiphar's wife tried to seduce him day after day. Through it, Joseph escaped saying, "How then could I do such a wicked thing and sin against God?" (Gen. 39:1-20).

Prayer of Application

Father, protect me from both the adulterous woman and from the smooth talker who from his pulpit of lies leads people on paths toward the spirits of the dead.

Pray for Adulterous America

30) Men do not despise a thief if he steals to satisfy his hunger when he is starving. 31) Yet if he is caught, he must pay sevenfold, though it costs him all the wealth of his house.
32) But a man who commits adultery lacks judgment; whoever does so destroys himself. 33) Blows and disgrace are his lot, and his shame will never be wiped away; 34) for jealousy arouses a husband's fury, and he will show no mercy when he takes revenge. 35) He will not accept any compensation; he will refuse the bribe, however great it is (Prov. 6:30-35).

Like burglary or theft, adultery is epidemic in America today. It is condoned on almost every secular front; in the daily press and in magazines; in novels, in movies, and on TV.

The commandment against adultery (Ex. 20:14) carried with it strict regulations against incest (Lev. 18:6), homosexuality (Lev. 18:22), and all kinds of perversions. Today, we see an almost complete collapse of these restrictions, as adultery in all of its forms has become commonplace. Unlike the thief in verse 30 above, who may steal to provide food for his family, the adulterer sins only out of his lusts and depravity.

But do not be deceived. What society condones, God still condemns. Men like Magic Johnson and Wilt Chamberlain, who brag of their sexual exploits, will ultimately tremble before the Husband whose fury knows no bounds. Let's join hands and fall to our knees in prayer for America and the other nations of this world who foolishly thumb their noses at God.

Scriptural Examples

Amnon. David's sin of adultery with Bathsheba continued to bear bitter fruit in the lives of his children. His son Amnon fell in love with his half-sister Tamar, then forcibly raped her. Amnon infuriated his father by his incestuous act, and Absalom, like the husband above, struck Amnon with fury (2 Sam. 13).

Prayer of Application

Dear Lord, as Isaiah said , "I am a man of unclean lips, and I live among a people of unclean lips." We also live among a people of unclean practices. Father, save us from our lusts.

My Personal Action Plan
....

STUDY QUESTIONS

1. Turn to Numbers 25 and read the chapter. What sorts of adultery were practiced by the people? What action did God take? Why do you think the sins of idolatry and adultery are linked? A hint: Who is the "husband" we desert in our idolatry?

2. In Genesis 2:18-25, we are told of the creation of Eve. What does verse 24 tell us about marriage? Who is to be involved in marriage? How many wives shall a man have? What does the phrase "one flesh" mean to you? (See Ephesians 5:31-32 for Paul's understanding.)

3. Job was a righteous man in God's sight (Job 1:8). Read Job 31:1. In what way did Job manifest this righteousness in his thought life? Compare that verse with Matthew 5:27-28.

4. Compare Leviticus 18:22 and 20:13. What does God think about homosexuality? What was the penalty in Israel for such activity? Who was responsible for its practice?

5. In John 8:2-11 we read of a woman found in the act of adultery and taken before Jesus. Who was missing from this scene? What do you think Jesus wrote on the ground that made her accusers leave one by one? How did He know?

PROVERBS TO PONDER
5:15-19; 6:20-24; 7:5-27; 9:17-18; 16:2

ONE TO MEMORIZE
The mouth of an adulteress is a deep pit; he who is under the Lord's wrath will fall into it (Prov. 22:14).

MAKING APPLICATION
My personal action plan to be sexually pure:

1)_____ 2)_____

3)_____ 4)_____

.Chapter Three.
A MAN AND HIS INTEGRITY

Part Four:

Purity of Speech

James says that "the tongue also is a fire, a world of evil among the parts of the body. It corrupts the whole person. No man can tame the tongue. It is a restless evil, full of deadly poison" (James 3:6-8). Our words display clearly what is in our hearts, and so the desire for purity of speech is linked inseparably to the purity of the heart.

"No man can tame the tongue," James says. Only God can tame it. Otherwise, the tongue spews forth its poison in the form of gossip, angry outbursts, lies, cursing, and recklessness. If we were to carry a tape recorder along with us as we go through our daily lives, what would we hear when we got home and played it back? Would it be pleasing to God, or would we be ashamed of what had come forth?

In this final part of chapter three, we will examine what the wisdom of God says to us about this evil organ.

Keep Close Rein on Your Tongue
He who guards his mouth and his tongue
keeps himself from calamity (Prov. 21:23).

When my brother and I were kids, we could not wait for Saturday afternoon matinees. The main feature was typically a "shoot-'em-up" western that usually starred singing cowboys like Gene Autry or Roy Rogers, and always had a scene featuring a runaway wagon. The heroine would be imperiled as the frightened horses bolted when the reins were dropped.

The hero would then try to get up on one of the lead horses to gain control of the team, or just grab the heroine and let the rig go over a cliff. Either way, a runaway team always promised calamity and kept us glued to our seats. The Bible tells us that the human tongue can be like those horses (James 3:1-8).

How do we rein in this troublemaker before we are carried over the precipice? First, we need to be keenly aware of the tongue's ability to dispense poison. Second, we need to speak only after careful reflection. Is what we intend to say true, pleasant, helpful, kind, and edifying? Does it submit to God's law of love? If not, don't say it! Ask God to help you control your tongue. He is more powerful than a zillion cowboys.

Scriptural Examples

Hezekiah. Hezekiah received messengers of the king of Babylon and proceeded to babble on about the great fortune he held in Jerusalem. His tongue brought great calamity on Judah. Isaiah foretold that all of Judah's treasures would be carried off to Babylon. That is exactly what happened (2 Kings 20:12-17).

Peter. When Jesus told His disciples how He must go up to Jerusalem and suffer and die and rise again, Peter rebuked Him saying, "Never, Lord! This shall never happen to you!" Jesus then rebuked the impetuous Peter for his foolish words spoken in haste, calling him "Satan" (Matt. 16:21-23).

Prayer of Application

Father, how often have I put my tongue in gear while my brain remained in neutral? Help me, Lord, to keep a close check on all my words, that they might always reflect glory to You.

Speak Only Good of Your Neighbor

The words of a gossip are like choice morsels;
they go down to a man's inmost parts (Prov. 18:8).

While I was in the army, I took a course in first aid. I learned that the most fearful wound one could suffer in battle was a bullet or piece of shrapnel to the stomach. Not just painful, the stomach wound usually caused a torturous death unless hospital care was at hand. Such are the words of a gossip.

In another sense, the gossip's words go down to the stomach as food for the man who delights to ingest them. They become a part of him. Ultimately they are poisonous and will corrupt the hearer as surely as they do the speaker (Ps. 15:3).

In the film "Bambi," Thumper the rabbit offered us this advice: "If you can't say anything good about somebody, don't say anything at all." Under normal circumstances, that is good advice. But there are times when we may have to warn our neighbor about an evil plot against him. Or perhaps that same neighbor's actions have been harmful to others and he needs our rebuke. In those instances, we must be absolutely sure of the accuracy of our information and that our motives are pure. Our words must seek the ultimate benefit of all involved.

Scriptural Examples

Joseph. In spite of the overwhelming excellence of his life before God, Joseph would sometimes come back from the fields and bring a bad report about his brothers to their father. As a consequence of Joseph's habit of tattling on them, his brothers built up resentment (Gen. 37:2).

Tobiah and Sanballat. This pair hired Shemaiah to convince Nehemiah to run to the temple and hide in fear of death at their hands. But Nehemiah realized that they were behind Shemaiah's lies and that they had hired him as a talebearer to bring discredit upon those rebuilding the city of Jerusalem (Neh. 6:1-14).

Prayer of Application

Father, let my lips speak only loving words of truth and health. Let me only say what is necessary about my neighbor, and then speak only words of peace, seeking the welfare of all.

Fight with Patience and a Gentle Tongue

**Through patience a ruler can be pursuaded,
and a gentle tongue can break a bone (Prov. 25:15).**

Back in the days of the French Revolution, when heads were rolling in the streets of Paris, a man across the English Channel was waging a different kind of warfare. His name was William Wilberforce, and his enemy was the English slave trade. For over 40 years, this devout Christian politician exercised patience and a gentle tongue, and won the battle to emancipate all of the slaves in the British Empire. What a contrast to the blood that flowed in America in our own Civil War fought over the same issue. And what a contrast to the way we men of this world typically wage our little wars.

My mind goes instinctively to 1 Peter 3:1-2 when I think of this proverb. There, women who are married to unbelievers are given instructions about how they are to graciously live with their husbands. Peter might just as well have quoted this proverb, applying it to unbelieving husbands. Nagging and belittling and arguing over doctrine never won anybody to the Lord. But patience and a gentle tongue have persuaded many.

Let us follow Christ's example, and whether the battle that rages around you is in your home, at your job, in your school, or at your church, use the weapons of patience and a gentle tongue. God is in control.

Scriptural Examples

David and Saul. While Saul was waging war with the tools of the world, David used a gentle tongue. At one juncture, Saul killed 85 priests of God in his vehement wrath. But twice when he had Saul cornered, David refused to take his life. Instead, David spoke to him with patience and gentleness. Saul was forced to confess, "May you be blessed, my son David." And David was blessed (1 Sam. 24:8-20; 26:17-25).

Prayer of Application

Dear God, I am often tempted to raise my voice in anger when confronted with wickedness and violence in the world. Help me to use the weapons of patience and a gentle tongue.

Seek a Tongue of Kindness

**Reckless words pierce like a sword,
but the tongue of the wise brings healing (Prov. 12:18).**

I have never been pierced by a sword, but I did put a telephone pole climber's spike through my foot as a boy, and I understand the pain that is involved. I have also received harsh words from a loved one that put a pain in my chest like that of a sword's piercing. It took several hours for the pain to subside. I pray that I will never hurt someone else like that. Words can cause deep wounds, and there are reckless people who use such words without compunction.

But God calls us to kindness (Gal. 5:22). Our first consideration must always be for the glory of God, and then for the welfare of our fellowman (Matt. 22:36-40). God has treated us with incredible kindness. How then can we treat other human beings with anything but the same? Shall we not rebuke others? Yes, we must rebuke them when necessary, but in kindness, hoping for reconciliation between parties (2 Cor. 2:5-7).

Scriptural Examples

Jesus. Our Lord was often the recipient of reckless words. Because He associated with people of low estate, and attended banquets and parties, the Jewish leaders falsely said of Him, "Here is a glutton and a drunkard" (Matt. 11:19).

Jesus. As He stood before the Sanhedrin, and truly testified of Himself, He was falsely called a blasphemer (Mark 14:64).

Jesus. They accused Him also of sedition (Luke 23:5) and of anarchy in plotting the destruction of the temple (Mark 14:58).

Jesus. But our Lord never spoke this way. He always spoke with kindness, except in moments of righteous rebuke (Matt. 23). Even then, His were words of truth, not slander. Our Lord spoke words of comfort and encouragement to the poor and the sick. We are called to walk in His steps.

Prayer of Application

Father, thank You for the example of Jesus, who spoke words of life and salvation. Help me, Lord, to treat all people with kindness. Not because they deserve it, but for Christ's sake.

Speak Appropriate and Fitting Words

**31) The mouth of the righteous brings forth wisdom,
but a perverse tongue will be cut out.
32) The lips of the righteous know what is fitting, but the
mouth of the wicked only what is perverse (Prov. 10:31-32).**

Wisdom has many sides. It's not just what we say that
shows forth wisdom, it's how we say it, when we say it, where
we say it, and to whom we say it. In Ephesians 4:15, Paul tells
us to "speak the truth in love." Our words should well up from
a heart that knows God, and seeks to please Him.

The wicked man will only speak that which is self-serving
and perverse, as he seeks to elevate himself at the expense of
his neighbor (Rom. 3:11-14). He will use innuendo and gratu-
itous flattery to serve his own purposes. The Bible teaches that
the natural man cannot help but sin in all he does, and bears
only corrupt fruit (Matt. 7:17).

But the righteous man speaks with gentleness and mercy.
He speaks at the fitting time, and does not blurt out in public
those things that are best said in private. The righteous man
seeks out the proper person to whom to speak, and does not
spread gossip. He does not slander others or belittle them to
attempt to show himself in a better light. His words transmit at
all times the sweetness and grace of his Savior.

Scriptural Examples

Daniel. What wise and fitting words poured from Daniel's
lips. In these verses, he told Nebuchadnezzar his own dream,
then interpreted its meaning to that king of Babylon. His words
were fearless, yet full of tact and grace (Dan. 4:4-27).

Nebuchadnezzar. But the foolishness and wickedness of
Daniel's listener soon was apparent as he did not repent before
the Living and True God. God took his kingdom, and sent
Nebuchadnezzar out like a wild beast (Dan. 4: 28).

Prayer of Application

Lord God, help me to speak only appropriate and fitting
words so that the sweetness and grace of Christ may be reflected in me and that He might be glorified in all that I say.

Beware of "Foot in Mouth" Disease

Do you see a man who speaks in haste?
There is more hope for a fool than for him (Prov. 29:20).

"Foot in mouth" disease is closely related to that common ailment "diarrhea of the mouth," and should be avoided like the plague. Its symptoms occur first in the mind. A sufferer begins to think that he knows pretty much everything about everything. Suddenly his mouth opens, and before he can get his brain in gear, out comes a gusher of words. No tourniquet or coagulant yet devised can stop the oral bleeding that ensues. On most occasions, these outbursts are followed by a reddening of the facial skin tissues as the infirmed's foot glides slowly from the ground to his mouth and becomes firmly imbedded between his upper and lower jaws. Those so infected should go on a strict diet of humble pie until the symptoms disappear.

I confess that I am sometimes susceptible to this disease, and am forced to ask God to forgive me. I pray that He is cleansing me of it, but just when I think I'm healed, it's b-a-a-a-a-ck. Do you have this problem? We need to weigh carefully the words that we speak, and avoid "foot in mouth" disease.

Scriptural Examples

Saul. In his conceit, Saul spoke in haste on the day his son Jonathan brought victory to the army of Israel over the Philistines. Were it not for the intervention of the troops, Saul would have put his son to death for eating a little honey (1 Sam. 14).

Jephthah. This judge of Israel rashly devoted to destruction the first thing that walked out of the door of his house when he returned from battle. Sadly, it happened that his daughter was first out of the door (Judg. 11).

The Lord God. The words of God are never spoken in haste, as if they had to be taken back. On the contrary, the words of God are flawless, like silver refined in the furnace (Ps. 12:6).

Prayer of Application

Dear Lord, keep me from putting my foot in my mouth by speaking before my brain is in gear. I am Your representative, Lord, and I need to choose all my words with care.

My Personal Action Plan

·······································

STUDY QUESTIONS

1. In Psalm 34:11-13, what does the psalmist say is the secret to loving life and living long? (See also 1 Peter 3:8-11.)

2. What does our Lord have to say about the tongue in Luke 6:43-45? Can an evil man's tongue speak anything but evil?

3. In Romans 3:10-18, Paul describes the natural man, the man without God. What does he say about their throats? Their tongues? Their lips? Their mouths? Why are these things true? (Hint: compare verse 18 with Proverbs 1:7.)

4. What does 2 Timothy 2: 24-26 teach us about witnessing to the unsaved? We must not _____, but be _____, instructing _____. What does verse 26 tell us about the reason for the natural man's situation of Romans 3:10-18?

5. What principle was employed by Nehemiah as he answered the king's questions in Nehemiah 2:1-5?

6. When Noah got drunk and passed out naked in his tent, Ham's son Canaan and his descendants got into a heap of trouble. Why? What did Ham do wrong? What should he have done? (Gen. 9:20-25)

PROVERBS TO PONDER
10:20; 13:3; 15:2, 4; 16:32; 18:21; 31:26

ONE TO MEMORIZE
Through patience a ruler can be persuaded,
and a gentle tongue can break a bone (Prov. 25:15).

MAKING APPLICATION
My personal action plan to allow God to control my tongue:

1)_____ 2)_____

3)_____ 4)_____

·Chapter Four·
A MAN AND HIS FAMILY

In the garden of Eden, God established the basic social structure of mankind – the family (Gen. 2:22-24). The family is the foundational rock upon which all other societal organizations stand. Nothing has changed over the years, except that in recent days the family has been under attack as never before in man's history. Sin and alienation from God and His Word are at the center of the family's downhill slide. As the family goes, so goes the balance of our social order.

As men of God, we are responsible to the Lord for the well-being of our families. It is a responsiblity that is not to be taken lightly, for the Lord will hold each one of us accountable for the various roles in his family (2 Cor. 5:10): husband, father, provider, and priest. The proverbs have a wealth of wisdom regarding these roles; only a small amount of which is included in this chapter.

We will look first at marriage, then at our role as fathers. Then we will examine what Solomon has to say to us about finances and about our role as working men, providing for the temporal needs of our wives and children.

.Chapter Four.
A MAN AND HIS FAMILY

Part One:
Marriage

If you were to ask your pastor what problem he sees most often, he probably would not have to think about it for long. He would quickly tell you of the pain he encounters in many marriage counseling sessions. Even in the church, where we have the advantage of God's Word and the Holy Spirit's applying it to our lives, marriages are floundering. Why? Because we have allowed sin to become a priority, rather than something to be avoided at all costs.

I could speculate that pride, sloth, and selfishness lead the parade of sins destroying marriages. But they would be closely followed by jealousy, greed, and drunkenness. Sin separates. It is the TNT that blows apart many relationships, particularly one as intimate as marriage. Love glues people together. Relationships thrive on a foundation of love (1 Cor. 13).

Someone has said that marriage is God's pressure cooker. That is, who you really are will be exposed in the marriage relationship. There is no place to hide. God's Word is also a mirror for us to see ourselves as we truly are. Let's look into it as we study these next verses.

Husbands, Lead Your Homes in Love

**15) Like a roaring lion or a charging bear
is a wicked man ruling over a helpless people.
16) A tyrannical ruler lacks judgment, but he who hates ill-
gotten gain will enjoy a long life (Prov. 28:15-16).**

Derek Kidner (p. 171) says that the tyrannical leader is
subhuman (15), stupid (16a), and short-lived (16b). That brings
to my mind a picture of old Archie Bunker, who in the 1970's
TV sitcom *All in the Family* ruled his household from a self-
styled throne of malicious accusations, thoughtless insults, and
self-indulgent despotism. But his program was not short-lived.
In fact, on the contrary, it set records for longevity. Why? I
believe one reason was that many saw in Archie Bunker their
own fathers. The show allowed them to laugh at some very
painful memories of their childhood.

The Bible condemns Archie Bunkerism. Just because God
has given us men the responsibility of leadership in the home
does not give us a license to be tyrants. We are commanded to
love our wives "just as Christ loved the church and gave
himself up for her" (Eph. 5:25). Was Christ a tyrant? Did He
come to bully the Church? No. He came to serve and tenderly
shepherd His people. He came to die for them and to save them.

Scriptural Examples

The beasts of Daniel's vision. Daniel had a vision of four
beasts coming out of a troubled sea. They represented the
tyrannical rule of four major kingdoms that were to come on
earth and which would ultimately be burned up (Dan. 7:1-12).

The seventy judges. At his father-in-law's suggestion, and
with the Lord's approval, Moses appointed seventy men to
help him rule the Israelites. Their qualifications? That they fear
God, be trustworthy, and hate dishonest gain. All the people –
the family of God – would then be satisfied (Ex. 18:21-23).

Prayer of Application

Our Father in heaven, in Your wisdom and providence You
have given to the man the role of family leadership. Help all of
us in that role to lead in love and in the grace of Christ.

Strive to Live in Peace with One Another

**Better to live in the desert than with a quarrelsome
and ill-tempered wife (Prov. 21:19).**

The desert that lies 70 miles east of my hometown can be a
very inhospitable place. There are lots of ways to die out there,
including dehydration, sunstroke, and rattlesnake and gila
monster bites. But even a hot, treacherous desert is better than
a cool beach house with a quarrelsome and ill-tempered spouse.

We can substitute "husband" for "wife" here. Wives do not
have a corner on being contentious and angry. There is perhaps
no situation on earth that is more difficult for a person than to
be the spouse of such a one. Even the desert will look good.

Our goal in marriage should be to live at peace with one
another. Husbands and wives should be the best of friends,
putting the other before self. It is in this way that we honor God
in our marriages.

Scriptural Examples

Nabal and Abigail. Nabal is the biggest jerk in Scripture,
with the possible exceptions of Ahab and Haman. Abigail was
a woman of enormous patience to be able to abide his contentiousness, stubbornness, and bad temper. David saw that quality in her and, following Nabal's demise, he took her back to
Jerusalem to be his wife (1 Sam. 25:2-39).

Zipporah. Moses' wife showed her bent for contentiousness in an incident involving her husband's religious practices
– specifically, the circumcision of their sons (Ex. 4:25-27).

Michal. This daughter of King Saul and wife of King David
contentiously chided her husband for dancing in the streets of
Jerusalem following the return of the ark of the covenant. She
called him vulgar and undignified. God rebuked her for such
contentiousness with barrenness for the remainder of her days
(2 Sam. 6:16; 20-23).

Prayer of Application

Dear Father, give us attitudes that reflect the humility and
the love of Christ. Help us to avoid quarrelling and strife, and
instead to seek peace and pursue it, making it a top priority.

Choose Your Wife with Great Care

**He who finds a wife finds what is good
and receives favor from the Lord (Prov. 18:22).**

The key to this proverb is that a good wife or a good husband – one who will provide mutual support, encouragement, sympathy, and love – is from the Lord's favor. A wife or husband who does not do these things is not necessarily good at all, and in fact can make his or her spouse miserable.

How does one go about getting this favor from God? First of all, through prayer (Gen. 24:12-14), the medium God has given us to request blessings from Him. Second, we may receive a good spouse through the wisdom God gives us in His Word. We should marry only in the Lord and avoid being unequally yoked with unbelievers (1 Cor. 7:39). Third, we should be careful not to rely too much upon the physical attractiveness of a potential partner, but rather seek out qualities that may be seen in godly men and women in Scripture. Finally, as married people, we should always seek to bless our partner in all things, as heirs together of God's gracious gift of life (1 Pet. 3:7).

Scriptural Examples

Manoah's wife. This woman, whose name Scripture does not give us, was the mother of Samson and a blessing to her husband. When the angel of the Lord promised her a son, Manoah was afraid because they had seen God face-to-face. His wife calmed him with words of comfort and wisdom (Judg. 13:1-14:3).

Job's wife. In contrast, this godly man had a foolish wife. As her husband sat stricken in affliction, she urged him to "curse God and die" (Job 2:9-10).

Boaz' wife. For me, Ruth is the finest example of womanhood in the Old Testament. Her loyalty, simplicity, beauty of soul, humility, obedience, faith, and love are exemplary (the Book of Ruth).

Prayer of Application

Heavenly Father, help those seeking wives to do so prayerfully and with a sound mind, relying on You and Your Word. Thank You for my wife, who is truly a gift of Your grace.

Nip Strife in the Bud

**Starting a quarrel is like breaching a dam;
so drop the matter before a dispute breaks out (Prov. 17:14).**

I think of the young man in Holland with his finger in a dike that had sprung a leak. His finger, in effect, was keeping the entire North Atlantic out of the fields of his homeland. Were a small hole to be left unattended, it would increasingly widen until the whole dike was breached and the land was flooded.

The proper time to correct a relational problem is at the beginning of the problem. The longer it is allowed to fester, the more serious it becomes. A phrase that I like says that we should "keep short accounts." This is particularly important in the context of marriage. We should not let the sun go down on our anger (Eph. 4:26). To the good advice to "kiss and make up" should be added this: "And do it quickly."

Scriptural Examples

Abram and Lot. Abram's herdsmen argued with Lot's about space to graze their herds. So Abram suggested a peaceful plan to part company. Lot chose first, and took the plain near Sodom, while Abram stuck to the hill country (Gen. 13:8-9).

Israel and Sihon. Israel sent an envoy to the Amorites, seeking passage through their country. Sihon, the Amorite king, refused and attacked the Israelites, only to be soundly defeated. He could have saved himself much trouble and anguish by simply fulfilling their request (Num. 21:21-24).

The disciples and Jesus. The disciples had been arguing about who would be greatest among them. Jesus defused the argument quickly by telling them that whoever wanted to be first among them must be the servant of all (Mark 9:33-35).

Paul and Barnabas. These great men argued about taking Mark with them on a journey. Ultimately peace was restored, even though it meant parting company (Acts 15:36-40).

Prayer of Application

Help me, Lord, to solve my relational problems with others quickly, and before they get too large and out of control. Particularly help my marriage, where the stakes are so high.

Seek Harmony in Your Family

He who brings trouble on his family will inherit only wind, and the fool will be servant to the wise (Prov. 11:29).

To cause division in the home is to inherit the wind of the fool, not the blessings of the wise. The common denominator of unity is love, while the common denominator of division is sin. Sin always causes division as surely as the love that Jesus teaches us brings peace and harmony.

A short time ago in my hometown, a young police officer was shot to death while responding to a domestic violence situation. Violence in families is now a common occurrence throughout America, and can be directly attributed to sin. Drug and alcohol abuse, adultery, and slothfulness are just a few of the sins that torment the American home.

The Christian family, both in the home and in the church body, is to be a place of peace, rest, and sanctity. Harmony is to be protected and encouraged. Selfishness, pride, gossip, envy, covetousness, and the like are great dividing principles. Love, joy, longsuffering, gentleness, kindness, and the fruits of the Spirit like them are the principles of peace (Gal. 5:19-6:2).

Scriptural Examples

Korah. His foolish murmuring against the Lord and his complaining of the leadership of Moses and Aaron brought death to Korah and his entire family as God opened the ground under their tents and swallowed them up (Num. 16:1-33).

Achan. Like Korah, this man also foolishly destroyed his own family. God had directed that all of the spoils of Jericho be reserved for Himself, but Achan covetously hid some of the plunder in his tent (Josh. 7:11-25).

Cornelius. This Roman centurion feared God and gave generously to those in need. His entire family was blessed with the ultimate gift of God's salvation (Acts 10:1).

Prayer of Application

Merciful heavenly Father, may I manifest the fruit of Your Spirit as I seek to live out my new life in Christ, to the end that there would be unity in my home and in the body of believers.

Know the Ultimate Joy of Sex

15) Drink water from your own cistern, running water from your own well. 16) Should your springs overflow in the streets, your streams of water in the public squares? 17) Let them be yours alone, never to be shared with strangers. 18) May your fountain be blessed, and may you rejoice in the wife of your youth. 19) A loving doe, a graceful deer – may her breasts satisfy you always, may you ever be captivated by her love (Prov. 5:15-19).

Recently, the Mississippi and its tributaries flooded the upper Midwest states and floodwaters tainted with sewage flowed in the streets. God is telling us here that adultery is like that, when a man rejects the sanctity of his home.

In the marriage covenant, God has provided us with a picture of Christ and His Church. It is to be a relationship marked by deep intimacy and a nakedness before one another in both body and soul. What a wonderful gift to mankind marriage is and what a major error it is to violate its exclusivity.

Husbands, rejoice with the wife of your youth (Deut. 24:5), regarding her as God's gift to you (Prov. 19:14), and cherishing her with gentleness and purity. Be satisfied with one another as your bodies merge into one (Gen. 2:24) and each heart seeks the highest good for the other. Only in that kind of relationship may the true joy of sexual intercourse be known.

Scriptural Examples

The loving couple. Verse 19 here contains language reminiscent of another place in Scripture: the Song of Solomon. In it, a couple who is very much in love finds great pleasure in their romance. For many years, the erotic language there describing the sexual delights of marriage was held by many to be taboo. But its graceful descriptions lift married love to a highly elevated plane and remind us that God meant the marriage bed to be a source of joy and wonder.

Prayer of Application

Dear God, bless our marriages and help us to remember our vows to You. Thank You for the intimacy between husbands and wives, and for its metaphor of Christ and His bride.

106 Proverbs *for* Promise Keeping

My Personal Action Plan

STUDY QUESTIONS

1. Read Genesis 18:20-19:26 for the sordid details of the story of
    Sodom. In 2 Peter 2:6-9, what are we told about the condition
    of Lot's soul? Why do you think he kept his family in Sodom
    in the midst of its filthiness? Why do you think Mrs. Lot turned
    back toward Sodom? (Hint: Turn to Luke 17:29-32 for Jesus'
    reading on it.) How is her sin like that of Eve in Genesis 3:1-6?
    In Genesis 19:30-38 we are told about Lot's incest. Where do
    you think Lot's daughters picked up such sinful ideas?

2. Genesis 2:24 is reiterated by Jesus in Matthew 19:5. Notice
    that the man is to leave his mother and father. In what ways
    should a man leave his mom and dad? What do you think
    "one flesh" means? (Hint: See 1 Cor. 6:15-20 and Eph. 5:29-32.)

3. In Ephesians 5:25-30, Paul gives instructions to husbands
    about how we are to treat our wives. In what ways do you
    think our love for our wives is like Christ's love for His
    Church? What practical things can we husbands do to live out
    Paul's instruction day by day?

PROVERBS TO PONDER
12:4; 14:1; 16:32; 19:13-14; 22:10; 27:15-16

ONE TO MEMORIZE
He who finds a wife finds what is good
and receives favor from the Lord (Prov. 18:22).

MAKING APPLICATION
My personal action plan to have a marriage pleasing to God:

1)_____ 2)_____

3)_____ 4)_____

·Chapter Four·
A MAN AND HIS FAMILY

. . . .

Part Two:
Fathering

I remember my dad with great joy and warmth. He died many years ago as I was just graduating from college, but my memory of him is as fresh as if I just saw him this morning. He was a fine Christian man and raised his sons in the discipline of God. But we were rebellious and sought our own pleasure, apart from the pleasure that is in the Lord. It was not until many years later that my brother and I came to know Christ. Someday soon, I will meet my dad again in heaven. What a joyful reunion that will be!

Many of you have fathers that are more like Archie Bunker of *All in the Family* than Ward Cleaver of *Leave it to Beaver*. The fathering taught by Scripture was not modeled for you as you grew up. But the Bible has much to say about your task and responsibility. Listen to it. Ponder the fathers of Scripture, both the successful and the unsuccessful. What made them what they were? In the next few pages, we will look at some principles that Proverbs gives us for successfully raising our children in the love and admonition of Christ.

Dedicate Yourself and Your Kids to the Lord

Train a child in the way he should go,
and when he is old he will not turn from it (Prov. 22:6).

The Hebrew word *chanak*, translated here as "train," is translated elsewhere in Scripture as "dedicate" (Deut. 20:5; 1 Kings 8:63). There is a sense in which we parents dedicate ourselves to the solemn responsibility of training up our children. Certainly, the emphasis here is on our responsibility.

I believe that Dr. J. Vernon McGee hit the nail on the head when he said, "The way the child should go is the way God wants him to go." From an eternal perspective, there are really only two ways to go, the ways of righteousness and wickedness. How do we ensure that our kids will go the right way?

There is no certain way, but I believe that God honors the sincere attempts of godly parents to bring their children up in the training and admonition of the Lord (Eph. 6:4). Parental training should adopt at least this three-pronged approach. First, children should be grounded in the Word of God. Read it to them. Teach them its stories. Tell them of the sin problem and its remedy in Christ. Second, as you admonish them in issues of sin, rebellion, and obedience, make the Word of God come alive by making practical application of it to their lives. Show them how the Word speaks directly to them.

Finally, and most importantly, it is imperative that you teach them by your own godly example. Charles Bridges says that "the child learns more by the eye than by the ear" (p. 404). The other two methods will be rendered ineffective if hypocrisy is seen in the teacher. Pray with your children. Confess your own shortcomings to them and tell them how God is working in your life. Take them with you to a Bible-believing church where they can meet other godly men and women. Dedicate both yourself and your kids to the Lord.

Prayer of Application

O Sovereign Lord, help godly Christian parents everywhere to dedicate their children to You, that they might give top priority to their instruction in righteousness.

Bless Your Children by Your Faithful Walk

**The righteous man leads a blameless life;
blessed are his children after him (Prov. 20:7).**

What you are speaks so loudly to your children they often can't hear what you say. If you talk a good game, but don't walk in a manner that conforms to it, you are not practicing integrity. Integrity comes when one lives what he says he believes.

There is a very foolish belief in some evangelical circles today that since we are no longer "under law, but under grace" (Rom. 6:14), the Christian can do anything he pleases and be accepted by God. This is absolute nonsense. While grace is vulnerable to this kind of irresponsible presumption, it never teaches it. We are "under grace" inasmuch as we are able to choose integrity over and against hypocrisy. By God's grace, and the indwelling presence of the Holy Spirit, we are no longer slaves to sin, but rather slaves to righteousness (Rom. 6:16-19). We fathers are called to lead a blameless life.

The father who has been truly called of God will want to walk in integrity. If he doesn't, his children will see through the ruse quickly. Bless your kids and live what you say you believe.

Scriptural Examples

Adam. Adam sinned against God in eating the fruit forbidden by God's commandment. Adam's children have paid for his rebellion ever since (Gen. 4:8-12).

Abraham. Abraham was a man of integrity who walked in the ways of God. He walked by faith, and God counted it to him as righteousness (Gen. 15:6). Abraham's faithful walk blessed his children after him (Gen.17:19-21; 18:19).

Job. Job suffered greatly but remained steadfast in his integrity. The Lord blessed the final part of Job's life, replacing his seven sons and three daughters. His daughters were declared to be the most beautiful in all the land (Job 42:12-14).

Prayer of Application

Heavenly Father, keep me in the way of righteousness by Your mighty hand. May my children see the evidence of Your hand upon me and be blessed, giving You the glory.

Observe Your Children Closely

Even a child is known by his actions,
by whether his conduct is pure and right (Prov. 20:11).

In computer lingo, we hear the acronym, "WYSIWYG." It stands for "What You See Is What You Get." What you see on the screen will be duplicated when it is printed on paper. Little children are like that. Not yet adept at masking their fears and feelings like adults, what you see is who they are.

A secular proverb says, "Large oaks from little acorns grow." A character flaw may begin as a little acorn. If left unchecked it will one day become a large oak. We as parents need to observe our children closely. When we see acorns of selfishness, vengefulness, pride, dishonesty, and the like, we need to stifle that trait's growth by discipline and fervent prayer before it forms into a settled habit.

Conversely, we are to encourage and to seek to strengthen character traits in our kids that will mature into large oaks of righteous behavior. Train up your children in the Word of God and watch as it does its transforming work in their lives.

Scriptural Examples

Jacob. Jacob's character was seen very early, as he came forth from the womb holding onto Esau's heel. It was a glimpse of the personal ambition and deceit that would mark his later life (Gen. 25:26; Hos. 12:3).

Samuel. The Lord's hand was upon Samuel from his youth, as Samuel's words were without defect. All Israel recognized that he was to be a prophet of the Lord (1 Sam. 3:19-20).

John the Baptist. The Spirit's hold upon John was evident even from within Elizabeth's womb (Luke 1:15, 44).

Jesus. Jesus' messianic mission was discerned by both Simeon and Anna as they served in the temple. His character and holiness were evident from His youth (Luke 2:25-52).

Prayer of Application

Heavenly Father, help us parents to be discerning of the character traits of our children even from birth, then help us to raise those children in the fear and discipline of the Lord.

Pray for Your Children
**To have a fool for a son brings grief;
there is no joy for the father of a fool (Prov. 17:21).**

A fool is a man who does not fear the God of creation (Ps. 14:1). What a painful thing it is for a man of God to have a child who thinks like this fool. If only we could inject our kids with the truth, and have them become instant believers! But it does not work that way, as you well know. Ephesians 6:4 tells us to raise our children in the nurture and admonition of the Lord. Sometimes, even when we do that to the best of our ability, our children wander into the folly of unbelief. What can a parent do to find peace in the midst of such uncertainty?

First, be a godly father who practices righteousness in all your affairs. Do not be too harsh with your children, nor too easy on them, but bring them up in a godly home that exposes their formative minds to the truth of God's Word daily.

Second, recognize that if the Spirit is to come into your child's heart, it will come only as the sovereign act of God. The prayer of faith is your mightiest and most effective weapon. Pray without ceasing for your children.

Scriptural Examples

Hannah. Hannah prayed to the Lord for a son (1 Sam. 1:28). God granted her desire, and she turned him over to Eli to be raised in the service of the Lord. In 1 Samuel 2:1-10, we are given insight into Hannah's prayer life. She sought God's help in raising one of the Bible's most godly men.

David. David prayed that his son Solomon, as king over Israel, would have peace with his enemies and be successful in building the temple of God. He prayed that his son might have wisdom and that he might keep God's law (1 Chron. 22:9-12).

Job. This godly man and devoted father made it a regular habit to pray for his children (Job 1:5).

Prayer of Application

Heavenly Father, thank You for my children. I pray that as I am in Your presence through the ages, they will be there with me. I love them, Lord, and humbly ask You for their salvation.

Discipline Your Children in Love

**He who spares the rod hates his son,
but he who loves him is careful to discipline him (Prov. 13:24).**

Discipline in the home should always be done from the perspective of love, seeking to put the child on a path of righteousness and purity. It should never be done hastily or in anger, or with the intent of revenge. The reason for the discipline should always be understood by the child and the application of a biblical principle should be made. Therefore, the discipline of our children must begin with our own self-discipline. Most of us hate pain and flee from it. But discipline, while it may inflict a small amount of pain in the present, will prevent much greater pain in the future.

Every human being is a child of Adam and is born with a predisposition to sin. We as fathers must lovingly and patiently combine teaching with physical discipline, if necessary, to encourage in our children a life of reverence for God and for His Word. Begin early and do not falter. No discipline is pleasant at the time, but in the end it produces a harvest of righteousness and peace for those who have been trained by it (Heb. 12:11).

Scriptural Examples

Eli and his sons. Hophni and Phinehas sinned wickedly against the people and against the Lord. The Lord laid their sin at Eli's feet. He had failed to discipline them (1 Sam. 3:13).

David and Adonijah. Adonijah attempted to set himself up as king in place of his aging father. David had failed to restrict him or to interfere with his plans (1 Kings 1:6).

Our heavenly Father and us. God disciplines those He loves, in order to give us wisdom, to instruct us in holiness, and to set our feet on a righteous path. We should view discipline as encouragement, because God never disciplines those who just pretend to be His children (Heb. 12:5-9).

Prayer of Application

Heavenly Father, thank You for Your disciplining hand upon me. Help me to discipline my children in Your way of love with exactly what is appropriate for each of them.

Fathers and Children, Bless Each Other

**Children's children are a crown to the aged,
and parents are the pride of their children (Prov. 17:6).**

This proverb speaks to what should be and not to what always is. So often in Scripture, we see the son turning away from the instruction of his righteous parents, or conversely, the parents bringing shame upon their children. Here we see that a man's children's children are a crown to him. What a delight to be a grandparent!

God created the family as man's first social structure, an institution created for man's blessing and well-being. When a man and his wife leave their parents and cleave to one another (Gen. 2:24), a family is created. If God's will is such, children will come. Parenthood is a great joy, yet a profound responsibility. But blessing and responsibility are also implied for the children here. They are to honor their parents (Ex. 20:12), who in turn are to raise their children in the nurture and admonition of the Lord (Eph. 6:4). The Christian home should be a great blessing for all who dwell in it.

Scriptural Examples

Adam and Cain. Adam lived to see many generations of his son Cain. God would ultimately destroy them in the Flood. Cain was not a blessing but a curse for Adam. Neither did Cain glory in his father (Gen. 4; Jude 11).

Adam and Seth. God had promised a Deliverer to Adam and Eve, and although the first couple may have thought Him to be Cain, it was from the godly line of Seth that He was to come. Adam was surely blessed by Seth's children (Gen. 5).

Timothy. Paul spoke of the excellent witness and faith that lived in Timothy's grandmother, Lois, and his mother, Eunice, and which now lived in him. Surely Timothy was the crowning glory of their lives, as they were of his (2 Tim. 1:5).

Prayer of Application

Oh, Sovereign Lord, may I be a blessing to my children, raising them with love for You, so that they may one day say that I have been their glory. Lord, that will be glory for You.

My Personal Action Plan

STUDY QUESTIONS

1. Read 2 Kings 20:19-21:9. Then turn to 2 Chronicles 33:1-16. Godly Hezekiah had a son named Manasseh who became king at a young age. What kind of king was he? What happened to him? How did he change? Do you think his early training had anything to do with it? Have you had Manasseh's experience, as I have? What can we do to teach our children to avoid it?

2. Ephesians 6:4 tells us not to "exasperate" our children. In what ways might we commit this sin? Did your father exasperate you? What are its consequences and how might we avoid it in our fathering?

3. Psalm 127 is a short psalm about children. Verse 4 speaks of children as "arrows." In what way are children arrows?

4. Amaziah followed his father, Joash, as king of Judah. We are told in 2 Kings 14:3 that he did what was right in the Lord's sight. What reason is given? Another father of Amaziah is given in that verse. Who is he? Did Amaziah follow his example? Why? What didn't he do?

5. What might Ecclesiastes 11:1 tell us about being a father?

PROVERBS TO PONDER
13:22; 19:18; 22:15; 23:13-16; 29:15, 17

ONE TO MEMORIZE
He who spares the rod hates his son, but he who loves him is careful to discipline him (Prov. 13:24).

MAKING APPLICATION
My personal action plan to be the father God wants me to be:

1)_____ 2)_____

3)_____ 4)_____

.Chapter Four.
A MAN AND HIS FAMILY

· ·

Part Three:
Finances

Like an army travels on its stomach, so does a family travel on its ability to pay the bills. Financial matters play an integral part in any family's well-being and in the relationship between a man and his wife. If finances are handled irresponsibly, or allowed to deteriorate, problems will most certainly arise.

Finances are one reason why it is imperative that we only marry someone who shares our faith in Christ and His Word. The "mixed" marriage is difficult mainly because the priorities of the husband and wife are not lined up. Each person has a different view as to what is important in life, and, therefore, how much money should be spent, and on what. Additionally, the parties in such a marriage look at the source of their financial underpinnings differently. The Christian trusts ultimately in God and His Word, while the non-Christian looks to worthless idols.

In this part of the book, we will examine the Christian family's finances and draw some important financial principles from the book of Proverbs.

Even in Wealth, Be Dependent upon God

**A poor man pleads for mercy,
but a rich man answers harshly (Prov. 18:23).**

I was discharged from the Army and began my business career in 1964. I did not really like the "dog-eat-dog" business world from the beginning, but stuck with it because I had a dream of financial independence.

The poor man in the verse above is dependent upon the rich man, who has no sympathy for his plight. He does not listen to his pleas for help, and answers harshly. The rich man is selfish, which he thinks keeps him from becoming poor. How wrong he is.

The rich man fails to see that he is totally indebted to God for every dime he has (Ps. 145:15-16; Matt. 6:26-33). When he dies, he will take none of it with him. He will stand naked and penniless to face judgment (Acts 17:31). Then, though he may beg for mercy, he will not be heard (Luke 16:19-31).

In the years since 1964, I have seen that financial independence can be like a mirage that retreats as you approach it. When we think we've got it, we worry about losing it. We've just switched our dependence to a bank account. True independence, I have learned, comes from total dependence upon the Living God. He is our stronghold and refuge, our very present help in trouble (Ps. 46:1).

Scriptural Examples

The prophet's widow and her husband's creditor. This poor woman asked Elisha to help her. Her dead husband's creditor was coming to take her two sons as his slaves. Through the providence of God her sons were not taken (2 Kings 4:1-7).

Lazarus and the rich man. Jesus told the story of a beggar who sat at the gate of a rich man. They both died. Lazarus entered "Abraham's bosom," but the rich man entered torment in hell. His trust in riches became a curse to him (Luke 16:19-26).

Prayer of Application

Dear Lord, thank You for the freedom and independence I have in my dependence upon You. You have given me Your Word, that I may know You and Your provision for me.

Prepare for the Future in Diligence and Faith

23) Be sure you know the condition of your flocks, give careful attention to your herds; 24) for riches do not endure forever, and a crown is not secure for all generations. 25) When the hay is removed and new growth appears and the grass from the hills is gathered in, 26) the lambs will provide you with clothing, and the goats with the price of a field. 27) You will have plenty of goats' milk to feed you and your family, and to nourish your servant girls (Prov. 27:23-27).

Over 30 years have passed since 1964, and I do not own any flocks or herds, not even a single goat. I do have a modest portfolio of common stocks, but I never made it to my goal of "financial independence." I like to say that I could retire tomorrow, but only if I were to die next week.

The wealth of this world is fickle and fleeting (Matt. 6:19) and, in the final analysis, cannot be relied upon to provide us with so much as a cup of coffee in the future. We are to rely upon God as the ultimate source of all we have. He is absolutely reliable, and our hearts can rest content in the knowledge that if all our investments flop, our pension plan goes bankrupt, and the Social Security system fails, God will still provide for all our needs (Isa. 58:11; Phil. 4:19). But does this knowledge preclude us from being diligent about providing for the future? These verses pronounce an emphatic "No!"

Scriptural Examples

Jacob. Jacob diligently tended Laban's flocks, and then carved out of them massive flocks and herds of his own. When he returned to his homeland, he had plenty to take with him, insuring food for his large family and nourishment for his servant girls (Gen. 30; 31).

Boaz. Boaz personally looked after his flocks and fields. He exercised diligence in his work and in his provision for the future (Ruth 2:1-16; 3:6-13).

Prayer of Application

Dear Heavenly Father, help me to trust You only as the Great Provider of all things. But then help me to do my part in providing for my needs and for those of my family.

Put First Things First

**Finish your outdoor work and get your fields ready;
after that, build your house (Prov. 24:27).**

Whenever I read this proverb, I always think of the pioneer family who comes upon a plot of land and decides to settle down. They sleep in their covered wagon until they get the corn crop planted down by the river. Then they begin to build their home on high ground above the flood plain. But most of us are not pioneers. How do these verses apply to us?

Kidner and Ironside both see "house" here as referring to a family. They say that the verse is telling us to get financially and emotionally stable before getting married. That is exactly what the pioneer family was doing, although in another context. They planted the field so that they would have something to put on the table when they built a house for the table. They put first things first. They had their priorities straight.

Actually, the verse above could have read, "First, get your medical degree, then do brain surgery." Or, "First, get your high school diploma, then join the Navy." How about, "First, save the cash, then make the purchase." The principle is the same in all of these cases. Be sure you have what it takes to advance to the next step in your life, then go ahead.

Scriptural Examples

The tower builder. Our Lord told of the man who wanted to build a tower. He said that the smart thing to do was to sit down and figure out how much it was going to cost and then, if he had the cash, to go ahead and start building (Luke 14:28-30).

The church builder. In building the Lord's church the principle is the same: First, know that your foundation is solid, then build on it. Paul tells us that this foundation is none other than Jesus Christ Himself and the gospel of salvation through faith alone (1 Cor. 3:10-15; Eph. 2:8-9).

Prayer of Application

Father God, help me to get my priorities straight. Remind me daily that my first priority is to seek Your glory and righteousness. Then, all else that I need will be added unto me.

Get Out of Debt

The rich rule over the poor,
and the borrower is servant to the lender (Prov. 22:7).

Have you seen the bumper sticker that reads, "I owe, I owe, so off to work I go"? The American way seems to be to load ourselves up with a mountain of debt as we seek "the good life" here and now, not understanding its ultimate toll on us as we become enslaved to the payments.

Christian economist and financial advisor Larry Burkett includes this principle as a common thread throughout his advice to clients: get out of debt, particularly consumer debt or debt that has been encountered in the purchase of rapidly depreciating assets. He views those assets differently from a house, which should have a measure of price stability.

The Christian who has indebtedness beyond a modest or necessary house payment is seeing his money go to interest each month that could otherwise be put to work in the Lord's service. Our credit card debt then becomes a two-edged sword. It cuts us in the direction of our servanthood to the lender, and then in our lack of servanthood to the Lord (Matt. 6:24). The best way is to be debt free, if you can pull it off. That should at least be a very practical goal for every Christian.

Scriptural Examples

Slavery and the debtor's prison. In former times, and certainly in Old Testament times, actual slavery might be imposed on a debtor, should his debt not be repaid. In some civilizations, debtors' prisons were common. Jesus alluded to this type of prison in Matthew 5:25-26. We just have a different form of slavery today.

The Egyptians. God honors the payment of debt. While in bondage to this nation for 400 years, the Israelites were owed plenty. On leaving, they got repaid (Ex. 12:36).

Prayer of Application

Heavenly Father, help me to live within my means, giving back to You my tithes and offerings and being cautious in taking on any debt which could enslave me.

Beware of Hasty Shortcuts
**The plans of the diligent lead to profit
as surely as haste leads to poverty (Prov. 21:5).**

Early on in my real estate career, I tried to score hasty "touchdowns" by going after big deals that were risky although they appeared to be "slam dunks." Most turned out to be "strikeouts" (to complete my all-season mixed metaphor), where the only things slammed were my wallet and my foolish pride.

Life should be viewed as a long distance race (Heb. 12:1). Such a race is run aerobically. That is, a runner's lungs process the air he breathes and do not build up an oxygen debt. In the 100-yard dash, run anaerobically, the runners catch their breath after the tape. Running sprints in a marathon is stupid.

Just as we need to avoid "get rich quick" schemes, we also need to avoid the other side of the coin. We can study an opportunity so long that it vanishes. In so doing we may just be afraid, and excuse our fear by calling it diligence. Jesus tells us that we are to weigh the cost of what we do, including the act of becoming His disciples (Luke 14:28-33). Then, after deciding to move ahead, we should work our plans with energy, discipline, and patience, dedicating the results to the glory of God.

Scriptural Examples
Saul. Because he wanted a quick victory over the Philistines, Saul gave a foolish order that his men were not to stop and eat on the day of battle. This hasty command caused all kinds of problems in the conduct of his troops and, most importantly, in his relationship with his son Jonathan (1 Sam. 14:23-45).

The shallow soil. In this parable, our Lord described one of four soils as rocky and shallow. The seed that was sown sprang up quickly, but died when the sun scorched the plants. So it is with some who receive the news of the kingdom with joy, but fall away when persecution comes (Matt. 13:5-6, 20-21).

Prayer of Application
Oh, Sovereign Lord, help me always to count the cost before undertaking a major decision. And Lord, keep me from hasty shortcuts and help me to take the long view of life.

Be Secure in the Riches of Christ

**Whoever trusts in his riches will fall,
but the righteous will thrive like a green leaf (Prov. 11:28).**

As I began to study the Bible, I marveled at the foolishness of pagans who worshipped gods of wood, stone, and metal. What advances man has made, I thought, to rid himself of these idols of superstition and impotence. I was the foolish one.

As I grew in the Word, I began to see that idolatry has taken many forms in history. Today, it is still practiced throughout America and the world, even among professing Christians. In one way, the pagans were more enlightened than we moderns. At least they worshipped gods of gold. Today, we worship a paper god: the Federal Reserve currency, the almighty buck.

But God demands unswerving allegiance. To put any object, commodity, or person in His place is idolatry (Col. 3:5). Paul says in Philippians 4:19 that God will supply all of our needs through His riches in Christ Jesus. Do you believe that? Or do you just play the game of lip service, trusting instead in your bank account, stocks, real estate, or Social Security check? Trust Christ alone. Be attached as a branch to the Vine. His riches satisfy like no other, and endure to eternal life.

Scriptural Examples

Abraham. Abraham was one of the wealthiest men in the ancient world, rich in sheep and cattle, camels and donkeys, servants, and gold and silver. But all of his wealth he attributed to the gift of God (Gen. 24:35-36).

Job. Job was also rich beyond measure and knew God as the source of those riches. In the midst of his affliction, he said that he would trust God even if God took his life (Job 13:15).

The rich young man. This young man asked Jesus how to get eternal life. Jesus struck to the heart of his problem when he told the man to give up his trust in riches (Matt. 19:16-23).

Prayer of Application

O Lord, teach me to trust You for all my needs. I have trusted You for eternal life, why is it so hard to trust You for my day-to-day sustenance? Give me the faith of Abraham and Job.

My Personal Action Plan

STUDY QUESTIONS:

1. James 5:1-5 contains several principles about the accumulation of wealth. Do you believe they teach that wealth brings accountability before God? What had these men done that provoked God to anger? Are your means to financial gain–business, job, or investments–pleasing to God?

2. Jesus told a parable about a wealthy man in Luke 12:15-21. What had this man done that was displeasing to God? What principle does Jesus state in verse 15? In what does a man's life consist? In verses 22-30 what sin does Jesus warn against? What truth in verses 31 and 32 does He then state? Do you believe what He said? Do you practice it?

3. Look at Proverbs 22:26-27. What do these verses suggest about the undesirability of debt for your family's security?

4. Joseph is my favorite Bible character. In Genesis 41:31-40 he suggests a prudent business plan to Pharaoh. What was it? What does this example from Scripture suggest to you about one aspect of your family responsibilities?

PROVERBS TO PONDER
6:6-11; 19:2; 23:5; 27:12; 28:22, 26; 31:10-31

ONE TO MEMORIZE
The plans of the diligent lead to profit
as surely as haste leads to poverty (Prov. 21:5).

MAKING APPLICATION
My personal action plan to get my family's finances in order:

1)_____ 2)_____

3)_____ 4)_____

.Chapter Four.
A MAN AND HIS FAMILY

....

Part Four:
Work

A man's work is an important part of his finances. Work is also a large part of who a man is, as he employs his talents and gifts and seeks fulfillment of his desires and goals. Happy is the man who knows himself and has found work in a field where his interests lie, where he is challenged and helping others, and where he is fairly compensated.

Our work is a spiritual matter, as these next verses from Proverbs testify. God is extremely interested in our work. We are created in His image (Gen. 1:26-27), and part of who God is may be found in His working as Creator and Sustainer of all things (Gen. 2:2; Heb. 1:3; John 5:17). We are to do our work as unto the Lord's glory (1 Cor. 10:31). Therefore, we are to be diligent, avoiding all slothfulness and putting our employer's (or customer's) needs above our own.

Today's workplace is difficult. Times and technologies are changing rapidly and it's not easy to keep pace with them. But the principles of the Word of God are timeless and cut through technological advances of any age. Employ them in your work.

Do Your Work as unto the Lord

He who tends a fig tree will eat its fruit, and he who looks after his master will be honored (Prov. 27:18).

Back in my college summers I worked as either a laborer or carpenter. My dad would say to me as I went to work, "Make a profit for your employer today." I found that he meant if my hard work made a profit for my employer, I'd make a profit, too.

The wise employee who tends to his employer's needs will himself be honored and enriched. At least that's the way it is supposed to work. Books could be filled with tales of unscrupulous employers who failed to pay the worker his wages or who absconded with the company pension funds.

As Christians, we need to understand that it is our heavenly Father who signs our paychecks. Everything we have, or ever will have, comes from His hand. Somehow, we have lost confidence in the providence of God over all the affairs of men. But that does not make it less true.

What it boils down to is this: If you are seeking justice in the work you perform every day in your employer's service, or even working for yourself, look to the One True Employer to provide it (Col. 3:22-24).

Scriptural Examples

The fig tree. In order for a fruit tree to bear fruit, it needs attention. Jesus spoke of a man telling his servant to cut down an unproductive fig tree. The man begged to be allowed to dig around the tree and fertilize it. The owner honored his servant's wish and gave the tree one more chance (Luke 13:6-10).

The faithful servants. In this story, Jesus illustrates the rewards given out in the kingdom of heaven to those who have been good and faithful servants. We need to work for the reward that never perishes, laboring in the field of the Lord, for His glory and profit, and for our eternal joy (Matt. 25:14-23).

Prayer of Application

Oh, Father, whatever I do, help me to do it unto You and for Your glory. Lord, I thank You that every calling is a sacred calling and all labor has its focus in Your honor.

Deal Honestly with All Men

The Lord abhors dishonest scales,
but accurate weights are his delight (Prov. 11:1).

One of the greatest mistakes we can make in our Christian walk is to compartmentalize life. We must take the ways of God into every detail of our work and leisure activities and not just into our times of formal worship, study, and prayer. What this proverb tells us is that if you own a grocery store and you falsely weigh the tomatoes to get one penny more from a customer, it's not just bad, it's an abomination to the Lord. On the other hand, an accurate scale isn't just good, it's His delight.

Greed is terribly shortsighted. The love of money produces evil (1 Tim. 6:10) and ends not only in shipwrecked faith, but in all manner of sorrow and grief. If you are tempted to cheat, even just a little, pause and ask yourself, "Why?" See the greed that is there and forsake it. Instead, seek the path of the righteousness of Christ and everything you truly need will be supplied to you (Matt. 6:33). And, God will be delighted.

Scriptural Examples

Jacob and Esau. While it is true that Esau held his birthright in contempt (Heb. 12:16), he was nevertheless cheated out of it by Jacob, who was egged on by his mother (Gen. 25:29-33).

Jacob and Isaac. Then Jacob pretended to be his older brother. He prepared some tasty barbeque and put goatskin on his hands and neck to deceive his father, Isaac. By his treachery, he stole the birthright that was Esau's (Gen. 27:6-29).

Jacob and Laban. By skillful manipulation, Jacob later dealt deceitfully with his father-in-law, Laban, and increased the size of his own herds at Laban's expense (Gen. 30:31-43).

Jacob and the silver. In his old age, Jacob had been changed by God. He showed honesty with the Egyptian rulers by requiring that his sons return the silver in their sacks (Gen. 43:12).

Prayer of Application

Dear Lord, deliver me from any attempt to cheat others for monetary gain or for any reason. Help me to be content to have what You choose to give me, Lord, and thereby reject greed.

Be Diligent in Your Work

**One who is slack in his work
is brother to one who destroys (Prov. 18:9).**

In St. Augustine's *Confessions*, he painfully recalls when he and some other boys stole some pears. The thing that troubled him deeply was that he was not hungry. It was pure vandalism. Throughout our nation, vandalism is rampant. There are crushed mailboxes, graffiti, and broken windows. But what does this have to do with being diligent? The proverb says that the man who is slothful is a brother to the vandal.

In the world today, much more harm is done through sloth than vandalism. God has given each of us gifts and talents to employ. We need to honor God by diligently using them.

The same principle applies to our work in Christian service. We are called to diligence in worship (1 Chron. 22:19), the study of the Word (2 Tim. 2:15), obedience (Deut. 6:17), striving after perfection, (Phil. 3:13-14), good works (1 Tim. 3:10), in making our calling more sure (1 Pet. 1:10) – indeed in all areas of life.

Scriptural Examples

The wise and foolish servants. Jesus tells of a master who left various sums of money in care of his three servants. The first two put theirs to work immediately, and when the master returned, they both showed excellent profits. The third servant buried his in the ground. Then, he accused his master of injustice and excused himself on the grounds that he feared such injustice. He was cast into outer darkness (Matt. 25:14-30).

Apollos. This man taught boldly about Jesus. He was diligent in the study of the Scriptures and in the way of the Lord (Acts 18:24-25).

Onesiphorus. Paul prayed to the Lord for mercy for this man's family. He had shown great diligence in searching for Paul in Rome and in meeting his needs in jail (2 Tim. 1:16-17).

Prayer of Application

Lord, I pray that I might receive a real spirit of diligence in all of the tasks I am given to do. May I always remember to bring my brain to work, that I may use it as You intended.

Set Realistic Goals and Work Toward Them

He who works his land will have abundant food,
but the one who chases fantasies will have his fill of poverty
(Prov. 28:19).

A good farmer will have his whole year planned. He knows exactly when to plow and sow and harvest and mend the fences and feed the animals. He has daily, weekly, monthly, and yearly goals that he sets for himself and his helpers. Then he gets up in the morning with one thought in mind: to accomplish what he has planned. He sets realistic goals and then goes to work. Each day he accomplishes just a little, so at harvest time his family's table is set for another year.

The "one who chases fantasies" (or rainbows) believes that money grows on trees. A man moved to Los Angeles because he had heard that money flowed freely there. He got off the bus and saw a hundred-dollar bill lying on the sidewalk and said to it, "You're just gonna have to lie there. I'm not gonna work my first day in Los Angeles." This fellow will chase whatever looks promising at the time without regard for setting reasonable, attainable goals and then working toward them. As a consequence, his table is always bare.

Set for yourself worthwhile goals in your business, family, physical, and spiritual lives, then work toward them diligently. God honors goals and will take you places with them you never thought possible.

Scriptural Examples

Solomon and the temple. Inheriting David's goal for the construction of a dwelling place for God, Solomon finished the drawings, planned the work, and built it (1 Kings 5:1-6:38).

Paul. Paul was a great goal setter, and was undoubtedly the greatest church planter who has ever lived. How did he plant all those churches? One believer at a time.

Prayer of Application

Dear Lord, it seems so simple, but realistic goals are powerful. Thank You for setting the goal of the cross for Jesus and for His work in marching toward that dark yet joyous hour.

Don't Hire (or Be) a Sluggard

As vinegar to the teeth and smoke to the eyes,
so is a sluggard to those who send him (Prov. 10:26).

There is vivid imagery here. Vinegar will truly set your teeth on edge and acrid smoke stings and blinds the eyes. A slothful employee is like these distasteful elements.

A central principle of a successful business is to hire good people. Without able employees, your business is doomed from the start. We who are employers, or who hire employees, need to take this responsibility very seriously.

In today's society, lawsuits are common, so proper hiring is even more important. Firing those who set our teeth on edge or blind our eyes with smokescreens is becoming more perilous daily. Take your time in the process. Get a consensus from others on the job. Do not fill the position too quickly. Review résumés and check references. You cannot be too careful.

What are the spiritual implications of this verse? We, too, are "sent" ones, as Jesus sends us in Matthew 28:19-20. Are we vinegar to God's teeth and smoke to His eyes? Or are we taking an integral and productive part in the Great Commission for which our Lord has "hired" us? With God's help, let each of us follow Christ's command with diligence and avoid the path of the sluggard who displeases his boss.

Scriptural Examples

The Laodiceans. Christ addressed one of His seven letters to this church. They were a bunch of "sluggards" whom Jesus promised to "spew out of His mouth" (Rev. 3:15-16).

The reluctant son. Jesus told the story of a son who refused to go to work for his dad, but later went. The other son said he would go, then refused. How this latter young man reminds me of employees who promise so much in the interview, but deliver so little when the chips are down (Matt. 21:28-31).

Prayer of Application

Father, You have called me to be diligent in all things and to do the work to which I am called in a profitable manner. Help me to fulfill that role at my job and in the Great Commission.

Honor God in Your Work

Do you see a man skilled in his work (KJV: "diligent in
his business")? He will serve before kings;
he will not serve before obscure men (Prov. 22:29).

When we are introduced to someone, the first question
usually asked is, "What do you do?" Man's identity is often
tied to what he does for a living. Man is a worker, the creation
of a working God who established the sanctity of labor in the
first chapters of Genesis. There we read of God's own labor in
creation. Adam tended the garden and became the first scien-
tist as he gave names to living things (Gen. 2:19).

In the Roman Church of the Middle Ages, work was
divided into two classes. The *sacred* calling was to serve in the
Church, while everyone else did *profane*, secular work. But
Scripture does not teach such dualism. On the contrary, we find
that all work is sacred (Eph. 4:28; 1 Thess. 4:11-12; Ex. 23:12;
34:21). The curse following the Fall added frustration to work.

Throughout Scripture we see godly men honored by secular powers and communities for their diligence in business or
in the work of their hands. Men like Joseph and Daniel are
examples of how God honors the labor of our hands and brains.
We need to be faithful to God in the work that He has given us
to do on the job, at home, or in the church. We bring honor and
glory to Him by being faithful at that work.

Scriptural Examples

Bezalel and Oholiab. These men were filled with the Spirit
of God and given skill, ability, and knowledge in the crafts that
were used in the construction of the tabernacle, in its furnish-
ings, and in the priestly garments (Ex. 31:1-7; 35:30).

Joseph's brothers. Pharaoh put Joseph's brothers who had
special abilities in charge of his own livestock. These men
would serve the king, not obscure men (Gen. 47:6).

Prayer of Application

Dear Lord, help me to honor You in my work. I thank You,
Lord, that You have given me meaningful and fulfilling work
to do and that You have given me the skills with which to do it.

My Personal Action Plan

STUDY QUESTIONS

1. Solomon thought he knew a good man when he saw one. In 1 Kings 11:28, he promoted a man named Jeroboam. Why? What reward did he give Jeroboam? Now go back and read the entire context in 11:25-40. Was Jeroboam the man Solomon thought him to be? Knowing what you do, would you have promoted him? Why or why not?

2. Now look at some other diligent supervisors in 2 Chronicles 24:12-14. How did the men they hired turn out? Did the job proceed well? Did they bring the project in under budget? What did they do with the money that was left over?

3. What advice does Solomon give us in Ecclesiastes 9:10? What three principles does he associate with our work?

4. Our Lord speaks in Luke 12:35-38 of some servants whose master was away on a trip. What principle(s) may we draw from these verses that would be applicable to our work?

5. What do Paul's words in 1 Corinthians 9:7-11 say to you about fair pay? Profit sharing? Is your pastor paid fairly?

PROVERBS TO PONDER
16:26; 17:2; 20:4, 13; 22:13; 24:30-34

ONE TO MEMORIZE
He who works his land will have abundant food,
but the one who chases fantasies will have his fill of poverty
(Prov. 28:19).

MAKING APPLICATION
My personal action plan to improve the quality of my work:

1)_____ 2)_____

3)_____ 4)_____

·Chapter Five·
A MAN AND HIS CHURCH

Following the resurrection and ascension of our Lord Jesus, the Holy Spirit came in power at Pentecost and the New Testament church began. Meetings of the Body of Christ were held on Sundays, or the first day of the week, in honor of the Lord's resurrection on that day. But the first day represented much more. For centuries, the Jews had celebrated the Sabbath on the seventh day of the week, as they looked forward to the time when the Messiah would come. Now that the Messiah had come, there was no longer any need for believers to look forward to that day each week. So the first day celebrates both His advent in history and His resurrection.

Today, we, too, are called to remember the Lord's Day and to keep it holy (Ex. 20:8). The day is a reminder of God's rest following the Creation, an eternal day, and calls to mind our eternal rest in Christ. Its celebration is even more ancient than the commandment, as it goes back to the beginning of time.

How do we celebrate the Lord's Day today? Many believe that we are to do acts of kindness and mercy or only deeds that are necessary. Otherwise it is a day of rest and worship. One aspect of the Lord's Day on which most all agree is that God's people assemble to worship Him on that day. We do this in our church homes. In this chapter, we will look at two aspects of a man and his church home: a man's pastor and a man's responsibilities in church leadership.

.Chapter Five.
A MAN AND HIS CHURCH
....

Part One:
A Man's Pastor

Your pastor is a man called by God to be the focal point of leadership in the local church. As such, he is the servant of all (Mark 9:35). It is a very difficult job and perhaps an impossible one were it not for the encouragement of the Holy Spirit. Such heavenly encouragement may be manifested in this life by men such as you and me. How do we encourage our pastor?

The writer to the Hebrews says this: "Obey your leaders and submit to their authority. They keep watch over you as men who must give an account. Obey them so that their work will be a joy, not a burden, for that would be of no advantage to you" (Heb. 13:17). In verse seven of that same chapter he says: "Remember your leaders, who spoke the Word of God to you. Consider the outcome of their way of life and imitate their faith."

Notice first that we are to submit to their authority. This is a command to join a local church. How else can we submit unless we commit? I am afraid that many of us "play" church and do not take the command to submit seriously. Next, notice in verse seven that we are to imitate our pastor's faith. We encourage our pastor when we imitate his faith. Let's look now into the book of Proverbs at some other ways that we may encourage and bring joy to our pastors.

Be an Encourager

**11) A word aptly spoken is like apples of gold
in settings of silver. 12) Like an earring of gold or
an ornament of fine gold is a wise man's rebuke to
a listening ear (Prov. 25:11-12).**

We do not grow many golden apples near my home, but we do have golden oranges. However, the allusion here seems to be to apples of the precious metal gold. Perhaps they are set in a silver ring. The idea is that a word aptly spoken is like a precious and choice jewel.

With your permission, I would like to change the word "rebuke" in verse 12 to "encouragement," and to look at the verses in that light. Actually, rebuke is encouragement. When we gently rebuke someone, such as our children, our motive should be to encourage them to be their very best.

If you are looking for a job to do in your local congregation, why not set yourself up as president of the "Encouragers Club." There are no dues or by-laws and it is OK if you are the only member. All you have to do to get started is to find someone who needs encouragement and encourage him! Someone who you know is hurting may need a kind word and an assurance that you are standing with him. You could send notes of encouragement to the sick. Or you just might write about how you appreciate the other person. Use your imagination!

In the next proverb, we will look at those who should be number one on your list of people to encourage: your pastor and his wife.

Scriptural Examples

Boaz. Boaz noticed Ruth as she gleaned in his field and encouraged her to stay and gather much. He commended her for her love for Naomi and gave her his blessing (Ruth 2:8-12).

Barnabas. This companion of Paul was a great joy to him. Even his name means "Son of Encouragement" (Acts 4:36).

Prayer of Application

Heavenly Father, help me to encourage others. I know from my own experience how sweet a word of encouragement is from a brother or sister. It seems to breathe new life into me.

Encourage Your Pastor and His Wife

Like the coolness of snow at harvest time
is a trustworthy messenger to those who send him;
he refreshes the spirit of his masters (Prov. 25:13).

Harvest time is the hottest time of the year in many places. The faithful messenger is like a frosty snowcone on a day of harvesting. Doesn't that describe your faithful pastor?

The encouragement we receive from the faithful preaching of the Word of God is far better than a cold drink on parched lips. It reaches down deep into one's soul and refreshes like nothing else can. When we are going through times of trial, the Word is especially encouraging. Without it we might give up.

But you know your faithful pastor feels the "heat" for his entire congregation. When one of his flock is hurting, he hurts with them. When someone is in grief, the pastor grieves, too. He needs everyone's encouragement. And don't forget his wife. She needs a special portion of encouragement as she seeks to fulfill her difficult role in his life and in the life of the church.

Here is a short list of ways you can encourage your pastor and his wife, although I am sure you can think of lots more: (1) pray for them daily; (2) attend church regularly; (3) ask how you can shoulder some of the heavy load; (4) send them notes of encouragement; (5) remember their birthdays and their anniversary; (6) invite them out to dinner; (7) above all, imitate Christ in all that you do. They will then be encouraged as they see the fruit of their ministry being borne out in your life.

Scriptural Examples

Jahaziel. Facing a war with the Ammonites and Moabites, the Israelites and their king, Jehoshaphat, were encouraged by this little-known man (2 Chron. 20:14-17).

Priscilla and Aquila. This couple encouraged Apollos, a bold preacher of the gospel of Christ (Acts 18:24-28).

Prayer of Application

Father, thank You for the encouragement of my pastor and his wife. May I in turn encourage them and become for them what they are for me, the coolness of snow at harvest time.

Be Faithful in Your Service to Others

**Like a bad tooth or a lame foot is reliance
on the unfaithful in times of trouble (Prov. 25:19).**

I have been a businessman most of my adult life, and have had a few employees who were unfaithful. As long as things are going smoothly, everything's peachy. But bring on the tough times and these folks become like the bad tooth or the lame foot described here. Of course, bosses can be faithless, too, and fail to serve those under us as we should.

You never know the true character of a person until the chips are down – until trouble comes. Then, what's inside us becomes visible. God uses trouble in our lives to give us a glimpse of what is lurking down there in the recesses of our hearts. Often, it is not pretty.

But Christ calls us to obedience and to lives of service to one another. In a large sense, we carry out His orders in the context of the local church. Too often, however, we Christians want to be served, rather than to serve others. Then we are like the abscessed molar or the broken toe. Encourage your pastor by your faithful service to him and to others.

Scriptural Examples

John Mark. When Paul sailed from Paphos to Perga, John Mark left him and returned to Jerusalem. Later, Paul refused to take Mark because of his earlier desertion (Acts 13:13; 15:37-38).

David. In Psalm 55, David's lament focuses on a man he had at one time considered his close friend, with whom he had enjoyed sweet fellowship in the temple of God. He may well have had in mind his own sons, Adonijah or Absalom, who both turned against his leadership and tried to establish their own thrones. But God was also giving us a glimpse of a future act of faithlessness, where Judas would deliver his friend, our Lord, to those who would crucify Him.

Prayer of Application

Father, thank You for our faithful friend Jesus. And thank You for those brothers and sisters who imitate their Lord in faithfulness. Help each one of us to be reliable at all times.

Find Wisdom's Secret to True Riches

9) Honor the Lord with your wealth, with the firstfruits of all your crops; 10) then your barns will be filled to overflowing, and your vats will brim over with new wine (Prov. 3:9-10).

The "first fruits" (or tithes) were consecrated to God by the Israelites under the law of Moses. It was a testimony to God's mighty hand in bringing the nation out of the land of bondage and into the Promised Land (Exod. 13:11-14). The offering brought rich temporal blessings from God. But what about today? Do we tithe, and what benefits are we promised?

There are two sides to the question. While some say that the tithe is still in effect, others disagree. They argue that under the law, the Israelites were like children under a schoolmaster (Gal. 3:24 KJV), while the new covenant treats us as adults (Gal. 3:25). The matter is left up to the individual's circumstances and conscience. God no longer wants a mere ten percent, He owns it all, and the question is, how much shall we keep?

Unlike Israel, we are not promised worldly wealth. In Luke 16:11, Jesus makes a distinction between temporal wealth and "true riches." True riches bring understanding of God's mysteries (Col. 2:2); met needs (Phil. 4:19); strengthened inner beings (Eph. 3:16); an eternal inheritance (Eph. 1:7); and the wisdom and knowledge of God (Rom. 11:33). This is the bottom line: that we affirm our trust in God by generous giving to His kingdom. Thereby we know the true riches of Jesus.

Bless your pastor and yourself as you honor God by your faithful and generous giving.

Scriptural Examples

The poor widow. She put in only a fraction of what the rich were contributing, but Jesus honored her as He said that in her poverty she had put in more than all the others. She had given all she had. Should we do any less? (See Mark 12:41-44.)

Prayer of Application

Dear God, keep me from presuming upon the freedom that I have in Christ and forgetting that I owe You all that I am and ever will be. Open my heart and my wallet, that I may honor You.

Drink the Living Water of the Word

**Like cold water to a weary soul
is good news from a distant land (Prov. 25:25).**

When I was in college, I spent summers working on construction projects. On one job I was to dig wooden sleepers out of concrete with a pick. It was hot, dusty work, and to make matters worse there was a dry desert wind that day that took the temperature to nearly 100 degrees. I have never been thirstier. That drink of cold water at break time was the best I ever had!

Good news from a distant land is like that drink of cold water. Because it comes from afar, its refreshment seems to be magnified. It's news from home! But this proverb is not just a statement comparing a cold drink to good news from home.

The Christian's true home is in a better land, the eternal city of God (Heb. 11:9-10). And we are not without news from that wonderful place! It is the fountain of living water, whereby we are cleansed and prepared for our journey (Eph. 5:26). It is the living and eternal Word of God. Sit at the feet of your pastor and drink deeply from the cool, clear gospel reservoir. Take joy in the man who brings you the Good News and in the knowledge of the One who has sent it to you.

Scriptural Examples

The angels. What Good News was announced that first Christmas in the hills of Bethlehem! Excited and refreshed by it, the shepherds ran off to find the babe (Luke 2:8-16).

The Prodigal's father. What good news for a father to see his son coming home! He did not wait. Refreshed in his soul, he ran toward his son and embraced him (Luke 15:20).

The Thessalonians. The good news brought by Timothy was that the Thessalonians, who had been visited by Timothy, were standing firm in the Lord. Paul rejoiced and was refreshed by the news from his missionary field (1 Thess. 3:5-8).

Prayer of Application

Dear Lord, thank You for the Word of God that refreshes my weary soul and causes me to look up in expectation of Your deliverance. Thank You for my pastor who teaches me its truth.

Pick a Church Home and Stick with It

**Like a bird that strays from its nest
is a man who strays from his home (Prov. 27:8).**

The bird's nest is its protection from predators and shelter from the elements. It is for raising of family in security. So, too, is the Christian's church home a protection from the world's buffeting and the deceitfulness of sin (Heb. 3:13). We need one another and we need deep and continuing relationships that will foster mutual accountability and spiritual growth. To flit from place to place is to wreak havoc on God's church.

The central reason for the "wandering eye" of the ecclesiastical tourist is his preoccupation with being served. He is there on Sunday morning to be spoken to, complimented, entertained, and coddled. He gives no thought to what he can do for others in attendance or for the real purpose of being there – to worship the God who created and sustains him.

When searching for a church home, find one that has opportunities for service in areas where your spiritual gifts can be utilized effectively. If you want to teach, find a local congregation that needs teachers. Then stick with it.

What encouragement to the pastor who hears the words, "We're thinking about joining your congregation. Are there any opportunities to serve others here?" Be careful if you switch church homes. Be fully assured that the reason for your move is not selfish, or due to your desire to escape responsibility.

Scriptural Examples

Dinah. This daughter of Jacob wandered from her nest and precipitated a horrible massacre of the citizens of Shechem. The incident scandalized the name of her father (Gen. 34).

Jonah. Instead of going east to Nineveh, Jonah's wandering eye took him out upon a sea that he knew the Lord controlled. It took a large fish to get him back on track (Book of Jonah).

Prayer of Application

Father, thank You for the church home that continues to uphold me in prayer and fellowship. When I was grieving, You used the same brothers and sisters there to encourage me.

My Personal Action Plan

STUDY QUESTIONS

1. In 1 Kings 5:1-10, Solomon sent a request to King Hiram of Tyre. Did Hiram supply Solomon's needs? What part do you think Solomon's father, David, had in the story? How do you think this speaks to our need to make long-term friendships in the church? Are you in your church for the long haul?

2. Read Romans 1:11-12. What does Paul equate with spiritual strength in these passages?

3. We often hear of Job's three friends in a critical way, as his castigators and opponents. But they were also an encouragement to him. Turn to Job 2:11-13. How did they do this? What might we learn from them in encouraging the bereaved?

4. In 1 Timothy 4:16, Paul gives instructions to a young pastor named Timothy to watch his life and his doctrine carefully, and to persevere in them. What is "doctrine"? Do you believe it to be important? Is there any connection between Timothy's life and his doctrine? Discuss with others.

5. In John 4, Jesus spoke to the Samaritan woman about "living water." What is this living water? If called upon to do so, could you tell someone what the Good News is?

PROVERBS TO PONDER
13:17; 14:23; 15:30; 20:6; 26:6-9; 27:10-11

ONE TO MEMORIZE
Honor the Lord with your wealth,
with the firstfruits of all your crops (Prov. 3:9).

MAKING APPLICATION
My personal action plan to bring joy to my pastor:

1)_____ 2)_____

3)_____ 4)_____

·Chapter Five·
A MAN AND HIS CHURCH
....

Part Two:
A Man's Leadership

Perhaps you do not think of yourself as a leader, but you are. While you may not have many followers, there are those who are influenced by who you are and what you do. You are leading them just as surely as if you were the pastor or even the President of the United States! The question is not, "Am I a leader?" The questions are these: "Where am I leading others?" "In what ways am I leading others?"

As men we are called to leadership in the home, on the job, in the church, and in the communities where we live. It is a serious calling. How many people we each lead is based upon our effectiveness as leaders. People are drawn to leaders who reflect their own values and goals, who have a vision for the future, and who possess the energy to pursue that vision. God's leaders are those who reflect Christ. They pursue righteousness. They lead others by their service to others.

The proverbs selected in this part of "A Man and His Church" speak to us about such varied topics as procrastination and slothfulness; the sources of authority; exercising authority in justice, mercy, and truth; leading others in love; and the leader's expulsion of wickedness.

Let's Stop Making Excuses

A sluggard does not plow in season (KJV: "by reason of the cold"); so at harvest time he looks but finds nothing (Prov. 20:4).

It's estimated that in any given congregation, ten percent of the membership does ninety percent of the work. Only four percent of the members of evangelical churches in America tithe. No wonder we can't reach the lost for Christ, with the majority of so-called Christians riding their hot-air balloons of excuses.

We have here a picture of the would-be farmer who can't plow his fields because it is too cold. Frozen land is not the problem here. It's personal, not physical. He is just uncomfortable plowing on those cold March mornings. He's procrastinating. Come harvest time, he will look out at his fields and they will still be brown dirt and weeds. No crops will have grown.

For many of us, procrastination is a habit that needs to be overcome. Not only are our plans and dreams stifled by it, but it brings depression and guilt in its wake. Let's stop making excuses and get on with the work at hand.

Scriptural Examples

Aaron. When Moses climbed the mountain, he left Aaron in charge of the camp. The people began to party and Aaron made a golden calf. Aaron blamed his sin on the pressure of the people. He said the idol just popped out of the fire. Aaron is an example of our propensity to cook up an incredible excuse if a good excuse will not come to mind (Ex. 32:22-24).

Gideon. God chose Gideon to lead His people. But Gideon began coming up with excuses. He basically accused God of not being able to do what He said He would do (Judg. 6:12-17).

The unwilling disciples. These two men excused themselves from following Jesus. The first had to take care of his father and the second wanted to bid his family good-bye. They placed personal priorities above the kingdom (Luke 9:59-62).

Prayer of Application

Father, forgive me for making excuses instead of being about Your work. Give me the wisdom to establish priorities, Lord, and then to make my priorities Your priorities.

Leaders, Know the Source of Your Authority

**A large population is a king's glory,
but without subjects a prince is ruined (Prov. 14:28).**

For kings, or for anyone in a position of authority, there is only one source of that authority: the Lord God Almighty (Rom. 13:1). God sets up and tears down kings and governments. He does it in His church as well. We dare not forget it.

But a secondary source of authority also exists. Without the consent of his subjects, the prince is soon destroyed. History, if not common sense, should tell us this. Recall the recent coup attempt in the former Soviet Union. The coup failed because the people (and God) stood against it. Jesus stated it this way: "Every household divided against itself will not stand" (Matt. 12:25).

Jesus also stated this principle of leadership another way: "If anyone wants to be first, he must be the very last, and the servant of all" (Mark 9:35). That is, you must find out what your people need and then get it for them. He knew precisely what His people needed and He got it for them. Let those of us who are leaders become servants, even as Christ served us.

Scriptural Examples

Saul. The Lord rejected Saul as king because Saul failed to obey Him. Saul did not kill all of the Amalekite animals. He had also engaged in the sins of divination and idolatry and had built a monument to himself (1 Sam. 15:12, 23).

Absalom. This son of David attempted to steal the hearts of the people from his father, and then set himself up as king (2 Sam. 15:1-10). His power play was to prove unsuccessful and he was eventually slain by David's forces (2 Sam. 18).

James and John. Their mother asked Jesus to place them at His right- and left-hand in the kingdom of heaven that was to come. Jesus replied with the principle that whoever wants to be great must be the servant of all (Matt. 20:20-28).

Prayer of Application

Sovereign Lord, teach me to pray for those in authority over me and, Lord, when I am called upon to lead others, may I lead with the same humility that was exemplified by Christ.

Lead Others in Reverence and Righteousness

10) The lips of a king speak as an oracle, and his mouth should not betray justice. 11) Honest scales and balances are from the Lord; all the weights in the bag are of his making. 12) Kings detest wrongdoing, for a throne is established through righteousness. 13) Kings take pleasure in honest lips; they value a man who speaks the truth (Prov. 16:10-13).

God requires that kings, or anyone in authority over others, rule in righteousness and in the fear of the Lord (2 Sam. 23:3). A leader is obliged to seek God's wisdom, and to apply it diligently (1 Kings 3:9). The following four principles are drawn from God's wisdom in these verses:

1) In situations requiring a decision, the leader will weigh all the facts and reach a just judgment (vs. 10).

2) The leader will execute justice rightly, not showing favor to one party at the expense of another (vs. 11).

3) The leader will abhor all wickedness and will not allow the presence of sin to reign in his administration (vs. 12).

4) The leader will surround himself with faithful advisers and value those who speak the truth (vs. 13).

Such leadership is honoring to God and leads to stability and peace. Christ's reign over this world is established and upheld in absolute righteousness (Isa. 9:7). How can we subscribe to anything less?

Scriptural Examples

Solomon. He was given wisdom by God in unparalleled measure. In one incident, he rightly judged between two women who contested the motherhood of an infant (1 Kings 3:16-28).

Abimelech. Abimelech murdered the seventy brothers of Gideon and declared himself king. But God sent an evil spirit between the men of Shechem and Abimelech, which led to Abimelech's downfall and death (Judg. 9).

Prayer of Application

Dear Lord, anoint my leaders with a godliness and wisdom that helps them choose the righteous way, rather than the pragmatic or expedient way. And may I lead others in wisdom.

Exercise Authority in Justice and Truth

23) These also are sayings of the wise: To show partiality in judging is not good: 24) Whoever says to the guilty, "You are innocent"– peoples will curse him and nations denounce him.
25) But it will go well with those who convict the guilty, and rich blessing will come upon them.
26) An honest answer is like a kiss on the lips (Prov. 24:23-26).

Someone says, "Wait a second, I'm not a judge! I don't have any authority over people! How does this principle apply to me?" I'm glad you asked. Are you a parent? Elected to an office at school or church? Supervise others at work? A hospital volunteer? Virtually every person in the world exercises some kind of authority over others at one time or another. These proverbs are aimed at that rather large group of people.

From almost the moment we are able to speak, we humans know the words, "That's not fair!" We all have an innate sense of fair play, and when it is offended we get very upset. I believe God is calling us in these proverbs to a strict duty of fair play, without partiality, where the guilty party gets justice.

God wants us to be a people of justice and truth. Whatever your position or calling, honest and forthright dealings with those under your authority is always the best policy. In fact, an honest and upright policy is just like a kiss on the lips.

Scriptural Examples

Joel and Abijah. These sons of Samuel accepted bribes and perverted justice. The people of Israel were very angry and cried out against their unrighteous rule (1 Sam. 8:1-3).

David's oracle. His last words bring tribute to those who reign in righteousness and in the fear of God (2 Sam. 23:1-4).

Job. Job sat by the city gate in the place of judgment and was revered by the people. He said, "I put on righteousness as my clothing and justice was my robe and my turban" (Job 29:7-17).

Prayer of Application

Father, how often it seems that fair play turns unfair under the influence of sin. Help me to be fair in every way, particularly when You have put me in a position of authority.

Leaders, Govern in Love and Faithfulness
Love and faithfulness keep a king safe;
through love his throne is made secure (Prov. 20:28).

The Bible is full of examples of rulers who exhibited the antithesis of this principle in their administrations. From Pharaoh to Herod, many governments were characterized by egocentricity, idolatry, and wicked despotism. In the northern kingdom of Israel, there was not one king who ruled in love and faithfulness, and only a precious few in Judah.

David was such a king. Although a sinner and imperfect, David was a good king. He pointed to the coming Savior and King who has established an eternal kingdom in love and faithfulness, a kingdom made forever secure for its subjects. Soon His truthful and merciful reign will be extended over all the earth, as He returns to take His rightful place as King of Kings and Lord of Lords (1 Tim. 6:15; Rev. 17:14; 19:16).

As leaders in the home, in the community, in business, and in the church, we are to govern in this same love and faithfulness. We are to seek the highest good for all those under our charge, serving out of a heart of truth and mercy. In this way we will portray Christ's coming again in power to rule the earth forever.

Scriptural Examples
Rehoboam. His reign was not one of safety and security, but of trouble and warfare with his brother (1 Kings 12-14).

Artaxerxes. This Gentile king showed more reverence for God than did the wicked kings of Israel who preceded him. He commissioned Ezra to rebuild the temple (Ezra 7).

The king of Nineveh. Here also is a Gentile king who heard the Word of God and repented of his evil deeds, leading his people toward a more righteous way (Jonah 3:6-10).

Xerxes. Here again is a Gentile king who exhibited a high degree of love and faithfulness (The Book of Esther).

Prayer of Application
Dear God, thank You for men who rule in love and faithfulness. Bless our political leaders, too, that they will rule over this country in ways pleasing to You. Come Lord Jesus!

Leaders, Allow No Wickedness in Your Midst

A wise king winnows out the wicked;
he drives the threshing wheel over them (Prov. 20:26).

There is a lack of discipline in much of the visible church today. Many congregations do not follow the rules set forth in Matthew 18 and 1 Corinthians 5. It is a serious fault, for by allowing gross sin to pass unpunished in our midst, we allow the message of the gospel to be stripped of its power.

A few years ago I visited a church where a matter of church discipline was carried out. And it was on Easter Sunday! I had been a member of two congregations that had been torn apart as the rules of church discipline were disregarded. I was impressed enough by the exercise of God's rules of order to make that church my permanent place of worship.

The visible church is composed of wheat and weeds (Matt. 13:24-30), and in most cases, only the Lord really knows which is which. That is not our business. But in matters where the negative commandments of God are violated in the church, He calls the leaders to a plan of action that will either restore the sinner through repentance, or drive him out of the church. In either case, reconciliation should be our primary goal.

Scriptural Examples

The Corinthians. A man in their congregation was guilty of immorality in the taking of his father's wife. And they were proud of it! Paul said that they should have disciplined the man and removed him from among them (1 Cor. 5:1-13).

Ananias and Sapphira. In a very severe disciplinary action, God called this couple on the carpet for not doing what they said they would do. In fact, they died on the carpet (Acts 5:1-11).

Hymenaeus and Alexander. In 1 Timothy 1:18-20, Paul spoke of these apparent blasphemers. He said that he "handed them over to Satan" for their instruction and discipline.

Prayer of Application

Dear Lord, You have called our church leaders to give account to You for those under their care. Give them strength, Lord, to carry out Your will even when it is not easy or popular.

My Personal Action Plan

STUDY QUESTIONS

1. Daniel 3 tells the story of two different types of leaders. (a) Who is the first one we are told about? (b) What did he consider the source of his authority? (c) Was what he did for the good of those under that authority? (d) Whose purposes were being served? (e) Do you believe that he was right?

2. We are still in Daniel 3. Three men are brought before the king. Who are they? Do you think they thought of themselves as leaders? Now answer questions (b) through (e) from number 1 above for the three men. What can we learn about godly leadership from these verses? About God? Would you do what they did? Who do you think the "fourth man" was in verse 25?

3. In Romans 16, Paul sends his greetings to the leaders of the church in Rome. What did he commend Phoebe for? Priscilla and Aquila? Apelles? Tryphena, Tryphosa, and Persis? Gaius? Who did he urge them to avoid? Why? What were these people doing? What can we learn about godly leadership here?

4. Paul urges us to pray for those in authority over us in 1 Timothy 2:1-3. What is the goal of such prayer? What then is the goal of godly leadership? Whom does it please?

PROVERBS TO PONDER

12:24; 14:19, 34; 21:22; 28:5, 21

ONE TO MEMORIZE

A sluggard does not plow in season;
so at harvest time he looks but finds nothing (Prov. 20:4).

MAKING APPLICATION

My personal action plan to be an effective leader in the church:

1)_____ 2)_____

3)_____ 4)_____

·Chapter Six·
A MAN AND HIS BROTHERS

There is one sense in which all men are brothers, since all are created in God's image (Gen. 1:26) and since God's common curse (Gen. 3:16-19) and common grace encompass everyone who lives on the earth. But in a narrower and more profound sense, only those who by faith in Christ are sons of God (Gal. 3:26) are therefore brothers in Christ. What is our brotherly relationship to be like?

We will address two central features of our brotherhood in this chapter: unity and mercy. They parallel the words of Micah 6:8 that say, "He has showed you, O man, what is good. And what does the Lord require of you? To act justly and to love mercy and to walk humbly with your God."

Justice, mercy, and humility are qualities of character that we are to reflect toward all of our brothers – those in the world, and those in Christ Jesus. But it is in our relationship to our Christian brothers that the rubber meets the road. We are to be especially just, merciful, and humble before them. Galatians 6:10 says, "Therefore, as we have opportunity, let us do good to all people, especially to those who belong to the family of believers."

·Chapter *Six*·
A MAN AND HIS BROTHERS

Part One:
A Call To Unity

In His great high-priestly prayer of John 17, Jesus prays four times for the unity of believers (vv. 11, 21-23). Three of those times He prays that the unity of believers will be like that within the triune Godhead. In verse 23, Christ gives us the reason for His prayer for unity. It was "to let the world know that You sent Me and have loved them even as You have loved Me."

In looking at the visible church today, we see little unity. Even in many local congregations, real unity is slippery if it exists at all. In Part One, we will look at some of the reasons why that is true and what can be done to remedy the situation. I am convinced that our foundational problem may be seen in verse 17 of John 17. There our Lord prays, "Sanctify them by the truth; Your Word is truth."

I believe that the Christian church is divided today principally because of a low view of Scripture. People refuse to believe the Bible and to be sanctified by it. Let's not be like that. Rather, let's find out what God wants us to do and then go do it. How do we find out what He wants? Become students of the truth. How do we do what He wants? Pray that the Holy Spirit will sanctify us by that same truth.

Bring Unity in Humility and Righteousness

**32) If you have played the fool and exalted yourself,
or if you have planned evil, clap your hand over your mouth!
33) For as churning the milk produces butter, and as twisting
the nose produces blood, so stirring up anger produces strife
(Prov. 30:32-33).**

Augustine said that humility is the central defining charac-
teristic of the Christian. It is the mark of a lifestyle that leads to
peace and unity among brothers and the mark of the life of our
Lord and Savior Jesus. The opposite pathways of pride and
self-exaltation lead to anger and strife.

If you were to stand at the doorway to your local supermar-
ket and take a poll of the people coming out, you probably
wouldn't find one in ten who thought that there was any
connection between their disposition and lifestyle and the
strife they encounter in life. We are a nation of "victims" who
blame some*one* or some*thing* else. But only *we* are to blame.

It takes no talent to stir up anger. Anger comes naturally
to everybody. Rare indeed is the person who is not easily
provoked (1 Cor. 13:5). At the end of anger's path is trouble,
while at the end of humility and patience is peace and unity.

An interesting play on words is in verse 33. The ancient
Hebrews spoke of a man with patience as being "long of nose."
Their word for anger was literally "short nose." But we see here
a bloody nose, made so out of the raw material of sin.

Scriptural Examples

Job. The Lord spoke to Job out of the storm. Job was almost
speechless. He said, "I am unworthy... I put my hand over my
mouth." Job knew when to shut up. Do we? (Job 40:1-5.)

Sihon. This Amorite king did more than just open his
mouth foolishly. He waged war against the wandering Israelites. He was to suffer more than a bloody nose (Num. 21:21-24).

Prayer of Application

Dear Lord, those who walk in pride are on a collision course
with their fellowman, and more importantly, with You. Help
me to be an example of humility and the fear of the Lord.

Seek Unity in the Household of God

An offended brother is more unyielding than a fortified city, and disputes are like the barred gates of a citadel (Prov. 18:19).

Bitter splits have been witnessed in the church through the centuries, where brothers are offended to such a degree that they set up barred gates between one another and close the citadel door to reconciliation. But God's will for His church is that it should be unified, not divided (Rom. 15:5; Eph. 4:13).

Why has there been such disunity? The answer, I believe, is in a simple three letter word: sin. Major divisions can come as people turn away from the Word of God, stripping the Word of its authority. While many denominational differences seem minor, and even silly, sometimes pride keeps us separated.

How do we solve the problem? Paul says that the solution is in love (Col. 3:14). This is not love that seeks unity at any price, but the love that keeps short accounts, confronts in humility, listens carefully and humbly to the other man's position, forgives readily, and faithfully interprets the full counsel of God's Word, relying upon its accuracy and sufficiency.

Scriptural Examples

Joseph and his brothers. Joseph first offended his brothers by tattling to their father, Jacob. Then he inferred that they would bow down to him. Years later, by the grace and purposes of God, there would be reconciliation (Gen. 37:2-11).

Israel and Judah. This split in the house of God would continue to divide God's people for years (2 Chron. 13:16-17).

The men of Antioch. Circumcision sparked their debate. With the help of Paul, Barnabas, and Peter, reason and the grace of God brought peace (Acts 15:1-22).

Paul and Barnabas. Sadly, Paul and Barnabas also had a sharp dispute. It apparently ended with the brothers parting company and going their opposite ways (Acts 15:37-40).

Prayer of Application

Father, I pray that I might live in peace and unity with my Christian brothers and sisters. Help me to be a peacemaker in the house of God by humbly submitting to Your Word.

Seek Peace in all Your Relationships

**Hatred stirs up dissension,
but love covers over all wrongs (Prov. 10:12).**

Another way to state this proverb is: "Sin separates; love unifies." Sin separates us from intimate fellowship with both God and our fellowman. Love reunites in its perfect bond.

In a parallel verse in 1 Peter 4:8, we read that "love covers over a multitude of sins." Does this mean that love hides sin? No. While love never gossips about the sin of another, there are times when love sheds light on sin. In such cases, our goal is to be reunited with our sinning brother or sister (Matt. 18:15).

Our local church congregations should be models of unity. But we often hear of a congregation torn apart by divisiveness. God hates this (Prov. 6:19). Does this mean that we should allow essential doctrine to be polluted in the interests of unity? Never. Rather, we are to consider our brother first, submitting to one another in love, out of reverence for Christ (Eph. 5:21).

Scriptural Examples

Satan. Why did Satan seek to cause dissension between Adam, Eve, and God? Satan hated all three and opposed the purposes of God. By his hatred and lies, Satan stirred up dissension where there had been unity (Gen. 3:1-6).

The Creator. When Adam and Eve sinned, their bond of intimacy slipped away. They covered their nakedness with fig leaves, the works of their own hands. But God, in His love for them, covered them with the skins of animals, slain in anticipation of the One who would be slain for their salvation and eternal unity with Him (Gen. 3:7, 21).

The Corinthians. There were dissensions in this church caused by petty jealousy and bickering. As he wrote in Colossians 3:14, Paul urges us all to put on the love that binds us together in perfect unity (1 Cor. 1:10-13).

Prayer of Application

Father God, help me to be a true minister of reconciliation. In my congregation of believers, help me to be a part of the glue that binds us all together in the love of our wonderful Savior.

Do Not Criticize the Roles of Other Christians
Do not slander a servant to his master,
or he will curse you, and you will pay for it (Prov. 30:10).

In my business, we keep a notebook of letters from customers who compliment our employees. We celebrate these letters loudly. On the other hand, sometimes we get complaints. Although difficult to receive, these are really of more value than the others. Why? Because management is made aware of a problem and can take steps to correct it. But this proverb is speaking of slander, of half-truths, innuendo, and gossip that is intended to harm, not build up.

As Christians, we are each the servant of our Master Jesus Christ. He gives each of us our marching orders and each set of orders is different from the next. The Christian's servanthood with his God is a very individual relationship and we must be careful that we do not impose our own orders upon others.

Please understand that I am not talking about the "thou shalt nots," or negative commandments. I am speaking of the positive commands which are open-ended and to which every Christian must conform as he is personally led by the Spirit. Each part of the Body of Christ has a different role to play (1 Cor. 12:14-20). To criticize another unfairly may equate to slander in the Lord's eyes. After all, Jesus is his Master, not you and I.

Scriptural Examples
Abraham and Abimelech. Abraham complained to Abimelech about the latter's servants, who had seized his well. It was a valid complaint, and the two men made a covenant between them that brought peace (Gen. 21:25-26).

Doeg and David. On the other hand, this Edomite told half-truths to King Saul about Saul's servant David. For the awful consequences of his act, Doeg came under the curse of God (1 Sam. 22:9,10; Ps. 52:1-5).

Prayer of Application
Father, help me to realize that I am responsible to You for my own marching orders, not those of others. Enable me to give solid advice to my brothers, but never to criticize them.

Be a Peacemaker

**A hot-tempered man stirs up dissension,
but a patient man calms a quarrel (Prov. 15:18).**

Our very salvation comes as a result of God's being slow to anger (2 Peter 3:15). Patience and self-control are fruits of the Spirit of God (Gal. 5:22). So we who bear that Spirit in our hearts are called by Christ to be peacemakers (Matt. 5:9).

We often think, when confronted with an unjust situation, that we need to give full vent to our feelings and stand up for our rights. But God requires that we overcome evil with good (Rom. 12:21). We are to live godly lives in witness of the One who truly brings peace. Anger and wrath do not bring about the righteousness of God (James 1:20). We live a supernatural existence and we are called to reflect a higher wisdom than that of the natural man. We are called to lives of patience.

But how do we put this principle in shoe leather? First, we need to rely fully upon the work of the Holy Spirit in our lives to control our temper and anger. Second, we need to realize that God is sovereign in all things and that we can submit to the circumstances of our lives knowing that He will never leave us nor forsake us. Finally, we need to have firmly planted in our minds and hearts that a hot temper is a reflection of our depravity, and as sin, it does not bring unity.

Scriptural Examples

Abraham. When his herdsmen and those of Lot began to quarrel over pastures, Abraham suggested that they part company so that there would be pastureland for all (Gen. 13:7-9).

Isaac. Gerar's servants quarrelled with Isaac over the ownership of a well. Isaac moved his flocks to another well, then another, until peace was restored (Gen. 26:19-22).

Jephthah. He was driven from his home by his half brothers. Desiring peace, he settled in the land of Tob (Judg. 11:1-3).

Prayer of Application

Lord, You have called us to be reflections of You, and as such to be peacemakers. Help me to do this by acknowledging You as sovereign Lord and trusting only You for justice.

Open Wide the Gates of Love

He who loves a quarrel loves sin; and he who builds a high gate invites destruction (Prov. 17:19).

If you are like me, you hate to argue and will do almost anything to avoid conflict, unless your principles and convictions are being compromised. But there are people who love a good quarrel. They seem to flourish in strife, because they love it. These are the people of whom this proverb speaks.

These lovers of strife have as their basic problem the sin of pride (Prov. 13: 10). They build a high gate between themselves and those around them. Their superiority demands that everyone else see things their way, even though it may not be backed with the authority of Scripture. They are self-willed, not God-willed, and rarely resist any opportunity for conflict.

The Bible is very clear in condemning the sin of pride and its fruits of hatred, discord, dissensions, factions, and the like. Paul says that people who live like that will not inherit the kingdom of God (Gal. 5:19-21). As the apostle Paul commands in Romans 12:18, "If it is possible, as far as it depends on you, live at peace with everyone." Open the gates of love.

Scriptural Examples

Gerar's herdsmen. Mentioned on the last page, these men quarrelled with the herdsmen of Isaac over water rights. They were Philistines who seemed to love to fight, particularly with the people of God (Gen. 26:20-22).

The Benjamites. Benjamites from Gibeah raped a visitor's concubine, who subsequently died. The Ephraimite cut her body into twelve pieces, sending one to each tribe of Israel. They rose up against the tribe of Benjamin that had "exalted his gate," refusing to bring the wicked men to justice. Virtually the entire tribe of Benjamin was annihilated at the hands of its brothers (Judg. 19:22-21:25).

Prayer of Application

Lord, help me to overlook the small things that can add fuel to an argument. But give me the strength to confront the person who sins against me, in a spirit of love and restoration.

My Personal Action Plan

STUDY QUESTIONS

1. Read chapter 1 of Paul's first letter to the Corinthians.

   a) In verses 10 and 11, what is the main problem that Paul is addressing?

   b) In verses 12 and 13, what is said about the nature of the problem? What were they doing? What should they have been doing?

   c) In verses 18-25, Paul speaks of the "wisdom" of men versus the "foolishness" of God. What are these two things and what do they have to do with the Corinthians' problem? What is the principle on which God has founded His church? What human principles were undermining that foundation?

   d) Compare verses 26-31 with Jeremiah 9:23-24. What similarities do you see? Compare Jeremiah 9:24 to Micah 6:8. What three principles of unity are given in each? How do they differ? What can we draw from all of these verses?

2. In Mark 9:33-35 Jesus confronted His disciples with what question? What was the root cause (a five letter word) of their problem? What does Jesus say about leadership and unity?

PROVERBS TO PONDER
10:18; 12:16; 15:4, 33; 16:18-19; 22:8

ONE TO MEMORIZE
Hatred stirs up dissension,
but love covers over all wrongs (Prov. 10:12).

MAKING APPLICATION
My personal action plan to foster unity among my brothers:

1)_____ 2)_____

3)_____ 4)_____

.Chapter *Six*.
A MAN AND HIS BROTHERS

Part Two:
A Call To Help

Reflecting the Micah 6:8 call to justice, mercy, and humility is James 1:27: "Religion that God our father accepts as pure and faultless is this: to look after orphans and widows in their distress and to keep oneself from being polluted by the world." The call of Christ is not a call to climb an ivory tower or enter a monastery, and thereby separate oneself from the world's problems, pressures, and pain. Rather it is a call to jump into the world with both feet, and thus while we are *in* the world, we are not *of* the world (Matt. 5:14; John 17:14-15).

At the end of the 19th century, a liberal form of Christianity came on the scene which emphasized a so-called "social gospel." The social gospel sought to feed the poor and house the homeless, but at the expense of the Word of God and its gospel of salvation. Unfortunately, the evangelical church overreacted to liberalism by losing much of its mission to the "orphans and widows." But God calls us both to preach the Word and to feed the poor. One without the other is like an automobile without an engine. That kind of faith is not going any place (James 2:14-17).

Let's see what the proverbs tell us about justice and our relationship to those less fortunate in this world's goods.

Treat Everyone with Dignity and Kindness
He who despises his neighbor sins,
but blessed is he who is kind to the needy (Prov. 14:21).

R. C. Sproul asks this: "What is the one question to which everyone will answer 'Yes?'" The question is, "Do you want to be treated with dignity?" Every person is created in the image of God (Gen. 1:27). While sin has defaced that image, people deserve proper respect because of it (1 Peter 2:17). Christ came to seek and to save the lost, such as these (Luke 19:10).

We are often tempted to despise our neighbor who is poor or different (Prov. 14:20). But we must not forget that the gap between them and us is infinitely more narrow than is the gap between Christ and us. He made Himself poor, that we might become rich in heavenly things. By being merciful, we remember Christ's sacrifice for us, and so honor Him.

But another reason for mercy is here. We are promised that our mercy will bring us blessedness. Our Lord even compared acts of kindness toward the poor as commensurate with doing the same thing for Him (Matt. 25:34-40). The blessings of the Lord will abound to him who shares his food with the hungry, and provides the homeless with shelter (Isa. 58:6-8).

Scriptural Examples
Job. Job said that it was his business to be kind to the poor, to be a father to the needy, eyes for the blind, and feet for the lame. Job took up the cause of the stranger (Job 29:11-16).

Cornelius. This Roman centurion was blessed by an angel of God for his prayers and for his generosity toward the poor. The angel then sent Peter to visit Cornelius with the saving gospel of Christ (Acts 10:1-4).

The church at Antioch. Following a prophecy by Agabus, these people collected a generous offering for the saints in Judea and sent it via Barnabas and Paul (Acts 11:28-30).

Prayer of Application
Lord, help me to treat everyone with dignity, especially those who are poor in this world, serving them physically and telling them of the One who came to enrich them eternally.

Invest in the Poor

**He who is kind to the poor lends to the Lord,
and he will reward him for what he has done (Prov. 19:17).**

For those of you looking for a place to invest your money, what provides a greater return than investing in the poor? Your investment will not be insured by the U.S. government, but by the Lord God Himself. He is surety for the poor. But there are a few restrictions He imposes before He accepts your deposit in His CD (Certificate of Devotion). First, you need a genuine pity and open heart for the poor and dispossessed. Second, understand that the CD will not be liquid: you may not get your principal and interest back in this life. But get it back you will, and at great reward (Matt. 6:19-21).

Jesus prophesied that we would always have the poor with us (Matt. 26:11). The reasons are complex, of course. But one thing is sure: as long as the poor are with us, we are to declare our own personal war on poverty, not relying on humanistic governments, but revealing what is in our own hearts. Then, when we meet Christ on that day, He will say to us, "Come, you who are blessed of my Father, take your inheritance... For I was hungry and you gave me something to eat, I was thirsty and you gave me something to drink...." (Matt. 25:34-35).

Scriptural Examples

The Samaritan. Jesus told of a man who took pity on one who lay beaten and bleeding on the side of the road. The Samaritan bandaged the man's wounds, put him on his own donkey, then took him to an inn and paid the innkeeper to look after him. Jesus says, "Go and do likewise" (Luke 10:33-37).

The deacons. In the early Church, a dispute arose about the distribution of food to the poor. The disciples met together and selected seven men to serve as deacons. The deacons were to insure that the poor were properly cared for (Acts 6:1-5).

Prayer of Application

Father, give me a real heart for the poor and needy, for those who are homeless, and for those who languish in prisons. They need both human kindness and Your words of mercy and hope.

Beware of Shutting Your Ears to the Poor

**If a man shuts his ears to the cry of the poor,
he too will cry out and not be answered (Prov. 21:13).**

In my city, as in other communities across the nation, the problem of feeding the poor and homeless has become widespread. But our government's welfare system locks the poor into a system of handouts and provides little incentive or ability to find meaningful employment. Such welfare is a sinful system that concerned Christians should challenge.

I believe that the cry of the poor is not so much "give me something to eat," as it is "give me a job to do." Educational systems and standards should be established that will prepare those not currently employable for 21st century jobs. This is the proper way to permanently hear the cry of the poor: give them work to do that is honorable and fulfilling.

My church is active in a rescue mission downtown that gives food, clothing, and a gospel message to all who come. Other Christian works help the needy in our society. They should be supported with our money and our time. Beware of the proverb's warning. To shut one's ears to the cry of the poor will bring God's judgment. We will cry out to Him, but we will not be heard.

Scriptural Examples

Job and Eliphaz. Job's friend Eliphaz accused him of shutting his ears to the poor (Job 22:7) and ascribed part of the reason for the calamity that had come upon Job to that sin. Job was confident that he was innocent of the charges (Job 31:7).

The rich man and Lazarus. For years, the beggar Lazarus had lain at the gate of the rich man, who wouldn't give the poor homeless man the time of day. Both died. The rich man cried out from hell for Lazarus to put only a drop of water on his tongue. His cries for mercy went unanswered (Luke 16:19-31).

Prayer of Application

Dear Lord, make me more sensitive to the needs of the poor in our society. Help me to serve them, to the end that Your Kingdom will be advanced and Your Name honored.

Glorify God by Having Mercy on the Poor

He who oppresses the poor shows contempt for their Maker, but whoever is kind to the needy honors God (Prov. 14:31).

The Westminster Shorter Catechism asks in Question 1, "What is the chief end of man?" The answer: "To glorify God and to enjoy Him forever." And how do we glorify or bring honor to God? One answer is found in this verse. We bring honor to God by having mercy on the poor.

God has made both the rich and the poor for His eternal purposes (1 Sam. 2:6-7). Each is made in his Creator's image. The rich man often looks with scorn upon him whose lot it is to be poor, calling him lazy, indolent, and worthless. To be sure, sloth can bring on poverty (Prov. 20:4), but sloth does not explain the vast majority of the people on earth who are poor. Whoever shows them contempt also shows contempt for God.

Jesus came to this earth at the poverty level and throughout His life He walked with the poor. He brought honor and dignity to the poor through His ministry to them and even claimed to be as one of them: meek and lowly (Matt. 11:29 KJV). He said that to treat one of these poor brothers with kindness was to do that kindness for Him personally, an act that will carry with it everlasting rewards (Matt. 25:34-40).

Scriptural Examples

The people of Sodom. One of the many sins of Sodom was that she did not help the poor while she herself was arrogant, overfed, and unconcerned. Sodom died in a fury and lives on in infamy (Ezek. 16:49-50).

Dorcas. This godly woman whom Peter raised from the dead was known for her kindness to the poor (Acts 9:36).

Cornelius. This Roman centurion was greeted by an angel who told him that Cornelius' gifts to the poor had been received as a memorial offering to God (Acts 10:4).

Prayer of Application

Father God, there are many poor people in our community, many even without homes and in need of clothes. Help me to be a blessing to them, and in turn bring glory to Jesus.

Do Not Romanticize Poverty
**The wealth of the rich is their fortified city,
but poverty is the ruin of the poor (Prov. 10:15).**

When I was in college, a security guard who had been on campus for years gave us some advice. He said that we should "get a solid education, because without it the road of life is long and pretty much uphill." Looking back after almost forty years, the wisdom of his advice rings crystal clear.

The middle class in America is wealthy beyond the wildest dreams of most of the world's population. It is very difficult for most of us to imagine living with gnawing hunger as a constant companion. We need to thank God daily for our wealth, our homes, our jobs, and perhaps most of all, the freedom to pursue wealth and to fail.

There is a real sense in which the fleeting riches of this life protect us from very little. But we should not disdain wealth, or "embrace poverty out of laziness or romanticism" (Kidner, p. 87). Rather, if called to riches in this life, we should be careful to share them with those who are poor (Prov. 22:9) and to understand that wealth is the blessing of the God who calls us to accountability for its wise use (Matt. 25:36-40).

Scriptural Examples
The prophet's widow. This woman illustrates the condition of the poor who are largely unprotected from the vicissitudes of life. She cried out to Elisha that a creditor of her dead husband was coming to take her sons in slavery to pay his debt. Through Elisha, God met her needs (2 Kings 4:1-7).

The Shunammite. In the very next verses of 2 Kings, we are told of a well-to-do woman who was also a friend of Elisha's. However, even in her wealth, there were things missing that money could not buy. In her case it was a son, for which she longed. God allowed her to become pregnant (2 Kings 4:8-17).

Prayer of Application
Holy Father, help me to have mercy on the poor and never to criticize their plight. Bring me to a better understanding of their misery and never allow me to romanticize such misery.

In Wisdom, Find Compassion for Others

27) Do not withhold good from those who deserve it, when it is in your power to act. 28) Do not say to your neighbor, "Come back later; I'll give it tomorrow" – when you now have it with you (Prov. 3:27-28).

Not only are we obligated to seek kindness and mercy for our neighbor, we are to seek it in a timely manner. The man who says, "Come back tomorrow," is devious in hoping that the needs of his neighbor will somehow disappear, be forgotten, or that his neighbor will find help elsewhere.

The very foundation of wisdom, and of God's law, is that we love God and love our neighbor as ourselves (Lev. 19:18; Matt. 5:43-45; 22:38, 39; Luke 10:27; Gal. 5:14). This foundational commandment leaves no room for selfishness or procrastination. We are to seek the highest good for our neighbor, not as a secondary motive behind that of serving self, but as primary, and thus influencing all of our actions on the earth.

The wisdom that is of the world says, "Look out for number one" – yourself. Selfishness is the root of pride, which is the root of sin, which is the root of all of the problems the world faces. Only in the selflessness of living to meet the needs of others may we find the peace, joy, and fulfillment that Christ brings.

Scriptural Examples

The old man in Gibeah. This old man came in tired from a long day's work in his fields and met a traveler in the city square. He knew there were wicked men in his city just as there were in Sodom in the days of Lot. In kindness and true hospitality, the old man took the traveler home and fed him and his donkeys (Judg. 19:16-21).

Boaz. The law required that field owners allow the poor and alien to glean the leftovers of the crop (Lev. 19:9-10). Ruth, who was both poor and an alien in Israel, came to glean in the field of Boaz. He went beyond what the law required (Ruth 2).

Prayer of Application

Heavenly Father, help me to gain more empathy for my neighbor and to look for ways to be of service to him, particularly those who are my brothers and sisters in the household of faith.

My Personal Action Plan
....

STUDY QUESTIONS

1. Read James 2:1-5. What had these rich men done to deserve such words from James? What had they not done?

2. In Jeremiah 22:13-16, what does God equate with knowing Him? What were the kings doing in opposition to this?

3. Nehemiah 5:1-13 tells of a conflict within the people of Israel. What had happened? What do these verses have to say to us about treating our brothers in Christ?

4. Let's look at injustice and a town named Shechem:

   a) In Genesis 34:1-30, what specific injustice is committed by the sons of Jacob in Shechem?

   b) They turned around and committed injustice again near Shechem as recorded in Genesis 37:12-28. What was it?

   c) Next, it was Abimelech's turn to bring infamy to Shechem. What happened there as described in Judges 9?

   d) Read 1 Kings 12:1-24. A son of Solomon went to Shechem. What injustice did he plan there? What was the outcome? What did it do to the unity of Israel?

   e) In Hosea 6:9, what injustice happens near Shechem?

PROVERBS TO PONDER
15:25; 18:5; 19:4, 6-7; 22:22-23; 28:8; 29:6-7

ONE TO MEMORIZE
If a man shuts his ears to the cry of the poor,
he too will cry out and not be answered (Prov. 21:13).

MAKING APPLICATION
My personal action plan to reach out to the poor and needy:

1)_____ 2)_____

3)_____ 4)_____

·Chapter Seven·
A MAN AND HIS WORLD

For all its seeming complexity, the Christian life and its message are pretty simple. The Christian life is one that reflects the glory of the Father by following in the footsteps of the Son in the power of the Holy Spirit. Our Lord gave us these two commands: "'Love the Lord your God with all your heart and with all your soul and with all your mind.' This is the first and greatest commandment. And the second is like it: 'Love your neighbor as yourself'" (Matt. 22:37-39). Love for God ultimately manifests itself in seeking the best for one's neighbors.

The Christian message is called the Gospel. Put in its simplest terms it is this: Mankind is in cosmic rebellion against a holy God. Try as one may, there is no way for a person to pay the debt caused by this rebellion. The penalty for sin is death, the eternal fury and wrath of God. But in God's grace, He sent His Son to pay the debt by shedding His blood on the cross. To be forgiven and saved, a person must repent of his own efforts to please God and trust solely in Christ's provision for him. Christians are to take this message to a lost world. The Gospel is what is best for one's neighbor.

In this final chapter, we will look at the Great Commandment of God, the Great Commission of the Savior, and the Christian's walk in the world by the power of the Holy Spirit.

.Chapter Seven.
A MAN AND HIS WORLD

....

Part One:
The Great Commandment

As we discussed in the introduction to this chapter, the Great Commandment is really two commandments. The first is directed towards God; to love Him with all our heart, soul, and mind. It is carried out in part in worship, prayer, and personal devotion to our loving heavenly Father and to His Word. We discussed those elements of the commandment in the first chapter.

But perhaps the foremost way in which the first of these two Great Commandments is lived out in this life is in the second, where Jesus says, "Love your neighbor as yourself." That commandment will be the central focus of our study in this part of our journey through Proverbs.

Love Your Neighbor as Yourself

**28) Do not testify against your neighbor without cause,
or use your lips to deceive.
29) Do not say, "I'll do to him as he has done to me;
I'll pay that man back for what he did" (Prov. 24:28-29).**

Our principle here is also a direct command of Jesus that is found three times in Matthew (5:43; 19:19; 22:39), twice in Mark (12:31, 33), and once in Luke (10:27). Paul speaks of the commandment twice, in Romans 13:9 and Galatians 5:14, where he adds that it summarizes the entire law. James calls it "the royal law" (James 2:8). In Leviticus 19:18, it appears in this same context, that of not seeking revenge against another.

Why does God not want us to seek revenge when we are wronged by someone? I believe the answer is threefold. First, we do not know all the facts. We cannot see into our neighbor's heart and judge his motives. Second, our judgment is always perverted by sin in our own hearts. Romans 2:1 speaks of this tendency every man has to judge others for the same offenses he overlooks in himself. Finally, that same sinfulness also prohibits us from making the punishment fit the crime. We will tend to err on the side of harshness.

But perhaps the overarching reason for loving our neighbor is that we are called on this earth to reflect the love and mercy of God. We have no inherent "rights" as such. All rights are God's rights, so in any sin He is the offended party, not us. Therefore, it is God's right only to seek revenge. We who have been loved by God have been forgiven much. How can we not, therefore, wish what is best for our neighbor?

Scriptural Examples

Stephen. As the stones rained down upon his dying body, the first martyr did not seek God's revenge upon those who unjustly executed him, but rather sought God's forgiveness of their sin (Acts 6:5 - 7:60).

Prayer of Application

Our Father in heaven, take the desire for personal revenge from me and replace it with a genuine love for all. Help me to be a true representative of Your grace and mercy on this earth.

Seek only Good for Your Neighbor
The wicked man craves evil;
his neighbor gets no mercy from him (Prov. 21:10).

This proverb reminds me of a short story that was written in the form of a diary. A man moved into a new neighborhood and proceeded to destroy the relationships there in any way he could. Through innuendo, deceit, gossip, slander, and vandalism, longtime friends were at each other's throats. Marriages were destroyed and children were plundered. After the wreckage was complete, the man placed one final entry into his diary: "Time to move."

The wicked man "craves evil" in that he lives for himself. He does not necessarily act in the manner of my short story example, but even when he does something seemingly out of a genuine love and concern for his neighbor, an underlying principle of selfishness is at work.

Some self-esteem advocates would teach us to first love ourselves, then we will be able to love our neighbor. But the Golden Rule actually teaches that we are to give the same priority to our neighbor's well-being that we would naturally give to our own. We do not need to be taught to provide for our own needs. That just comes naturally. Only through the Spirit of God working through us will we learn to put the law of love to practice in our neighborhoods.

Scriptural Examples

Paul. Paul cried out regarding his own wickedness. The evil that he hated, he did, and the good that he loved, he did not do. He concluded that only the Lord Jesus could rescue him from his body of death, his sin nature (Rom. 7:15-25).

Nabal. This descendant of the righteous Caleb should have been more like his ancestor. But when David asked for food, he reciprocated David's earlier kindness with evil (1 Sam. 25).

Prayer of Application

Heavenly Father, help me to practice Your principle of agape love in all that I do, seeking the highest and best for my neighbor and expecting nothing in return.

Emulate the Unfailing Friendship of Christ
A friend loves at all times,
and a brother is born for adversity (Prov. 17:17).

I am reminded of the champion boxer who, as long as money and fame are flowing, has lots of friends. But let him lose his skills and his championship, and his entourage disappears. So it is with worldly friends.

But true friends love you regardless of your circumstances and are, in fact, born for adversity. Where do we find such a friend? One is right beside you. He is the living Savior. He says that he will never leave you nor forsake you (Heb. 13:5).

In light of Christ's unfailing love for us, what kind of friends and brothers should we be? We should emulate the One who calls us to reflect His love (Gal. 2:20). To visit a friend when he is sick, or when disaster strikes, is to represent Him. To share with our friends their joys and victories, as well as their sorrows and defeats, is to be the kind of friend that Jesus exemplifies.

Scriptural Examples
Joseph and his brothers. Even though they had sold him into slavery and hardship, Joseph loved his brothers with a Christlike love. When they came to Egypt seeking food, he opened his arms and received them with tears of brotherhood, forgiveness, and friendship (Gen. 45:5).

Ruth and Naomi. The young widow Ruth stuck by her mother-in-law and vowed to stay with her regardless of the circumstances or consequences (Ruth 1:16).

Jonathan and David. This friendship withstood the ravages of Saul's hatred and jealousy of David (1 Sam. 18:3).

John and Mary. At Jesus' request on the cross, John took His mother into his home to care for her (John 19:27).

Paul, Priscilla, and Aquila. These friends of Paul stuck with him when the going got tough, risking their lives (Rom. 16:3-4).

Prayer of Application
Father, thank You for the friend I have in Christ. Oh, that I would be more like Him and carry the message of His love to my unsaved friends who need His friendship so much.

Be Generous

**24) One man gives freely, yet gains even more; another
withholds unduly, but comes to poverty. 25) A generous man
will prosper; he who refreshes others will himself be
refreshed. 26) People curse the man who hoards grain, but
blessing crowns him who is willing to sell (Prov.11:24-26).**

In agricultural communities, a greedy man might buy a
poor farmer's crops for a low price, then withhold that supply
of food from the market. As demand increased in relation to the
shortened supply, the price per bushel would be driven higher.
The greedy man would then wait for the perfect time and sell
for an exorbitant price.

But the Christian is called to use God's system of econom-
ics. First, he is to recognize that God is the source of all things.
Second, God honors the man who shares generously of the
goods, talents, and money that God has entrusted to him. In
feeding the 5,000 and again the 4,000, Jesus showed His ability
to provide all the food the people needed. In God's economy,
there is no lack of supply. Someone has said, "You can't out-
give God." I believe that is true. God will richly reward the
person who steps out in faith and generosity, trusting in the
One who freely gives him all things (Phil. 4:19).

Scriptural Examples

The money changers. Jesus entered the temple area and
drove these men out. Apparently, they were taking advantage
of the worshippers by setting unfair rates of exchange for the
temple currency. Jesus' zeal for His Father's house matched His
distaste for those who made it a den of thieves (John 2:15-16).

The early church. The early Christians practiced great
generosity so that there were no needy brothers and sisters
among them. As needs arose, some sold land and houses to
provide funds for distribution (Acts 4:34).

Prayer of Application

Lord God, help me to understand that all things are provided
by Your mighty hand. Teach me to be generous to those who
are in need and to use my resources for Your kingdom.

Bless the Community by Your Faithful Walk

**10) When the righteous prosper, the city rejoices;
when the wicked perish, there are shouts of joy.
11) Through the blessing of the upright a city is exalted,
but by the mouth of the wicked it is destroyed (Prov. 11:10-11).**

There are many today who say that Christians are a plague upon society, not a blessing. They hate the moral law of God and would erase it from the public consciousness. Christians are being ridiculed for their stands against the evils of abortion and homosexuality, to name only two issues, by those who would call evil "good," and good "evil" (Isa. 5:20).

Throughout its history, Christianity has been a blessing to society. Hospitals, schools, and orphanages, as well as the rights and dignity of women and the abolition of slavery, are only a few of the areas where Christian wisdom, work, and prayer have made a difference. We need to get involved today in the political process by supporting those who are on the side of righteousness, and who know of its role in the stability and welfare of the community.

Bless your community by your faithful walk and involvement in the political process. Write letters or telephone your elected officials and other leaders. Stand against those whose wicked mouths would overthrow and not build up.

Scriptural Examples

Mordecai and Susa. The evil Haman plotted genocide against the Jews in Babylon. But Esther and her cousin Mordecai won King Xerxes' favor in the matter and Haman was hanged. Mordecai was elevated in the government and the people of Susa and all the Jews in the land had a joyous celebration because of the victory of good over evil (Esther 8:7-17).

Sodom. The sins of Sodom were many and are duplicated to the extreme in American society today. The city was not blessed by God, but was destroyed by Him (Gen. 19).

Prayer of Application

Father God, by Your grace enable me to be a blessing to my community here on this earth. Strengthen me, Lord, to work and to pray for those in authority, that Your will may be done.

Respect the Dignity of Others
**12) A man who lacks judgment derides his neighbor,
but a man of understanding holds his tongue.
13) A gossip betrays a confidence,
but a trustworthy man keeps a secret (Prov. 11:12-13).**

We all know people who love to hear juicy gossip and can't wait to spread it. They don't even consider whether it is true, or whether they may harm someone. They just open their mouths and out it comes. What motivates these people to act as they do?

As usual, pride is the principal culprit. A gossip wants to feel superior to his neighbor. By debasing his target, he thinks he is elevating himself. Gossip is cheap and fraudulent. The gossip may even reveal secret things that were given to him in strictest confidence, simply to gain this self-exaltation.

Gossip and slander are the safest ways to attack someone. To confront a neighbor directly is too perilous. How much safer it is to secretly sneak behind his back. We must be discerning of this foolishness and rebuke the gossip. To listen to gossip is to give credence to it. The gossip is a coward and only exhibits a low opinion of himself in his madness.

But the man of wisdom holds his peace. Why? First, wisdom implies self-knowledge. A man of wisdom knows that he is not superior to his neighbor. Second, wisdom brings the "love" principle. Love does no harm to its neighbor (Rom. 13:10). We are to love our neighbor as ourselves, and treat him with dignity. With God's help, may we act only in love.

Scriptural Examples
Tobiah and Sanballat. These evil men tried to frighten Nehemiah into thinking they were coming to kill him. They showed their lack of wisdom as they spread their lies (Neh. 6).

Judas. What a picture of some gossips! They kiss you when in your presence, telling you what a fine person you are, but stab you in the back when out of earshot (Matt. 26:47-49).

Prayer of Application
Dear Lord, by Your Spirit, keep me from listening to or spreading gossip. Help me rather to live by the law of love that seeks no harm for its neighbor, only that which is good.

My Personal Action Plan

STUDY QUESTIONS

1. The Lord established a very creative punishment for anyone found guilty of maliciously bearing false witness against his neighbor. Read Deuteronomy 19:16-20 to find out what it was. What might these verses tell us of God's ultimate judgment of men's hearts that is spoken of in Acts 17:31?

2. In Luke 10:30-37, Jesus told of a man who epitomized the law of love for one's neighbor. How many acts of mercy can you count that the man did on this one occasion? What did the other travelers do? Who were they? What excuses can you imagine that they might have cooked up so as not to get involved? By this story, who does Jesus say our neighbor is? What are we to do? Can you think of an instance where you have done what the Samaritan did? What the priest and the Levite did?

3. What does Acts 13:22 say about King David? How do you think 2 Samuel 9 exemplifies this quality? Now read 2 Samuel 16:5-13. What did Shimei say about David? What was David's response? How did his response prove the statement in Acts? In what other ways did the life of David show this quality?

PROVERBS TO PONDER
8:17; 12:19; 16:22; 17:9; 18:20-21; 25:18

ONE TO MEMORIZE
A friend loves at all times,
and a brother is born for adversity (Prov. 17:17).

MAKING APPLICATION
My personal action plan to love my neighbor as myself:

1)_____ 2)_____

3)_____ 4)_____

.Chapter Seven.
A MAN AND HIS WORLD

....

Part Two:

The Great Commission

Just as the Great Commandment comes to us in two interrelated parts, so does the Great Commission. In Matthew 28:19-20, Jesus says, "Therefore go and make disciples of all nations, baptizing them in the name of the Father and of the Son and of the Holy Spirit, and teaching them to obey everything I have commanded you. And surely I am with you always, to the very end of the age."

First there is a command to "go and make disciples of all nations." Then he says, "teaching them to obey everything I have commanded you." This part of the book is primarily concerned with the first part of the Great Commission. The entire book is concerned with the second part. Christ is our great Prophet, Priest, and King. He is Prophet in that He teaches us by His Word. He is Priest in that He intercedes for us in heaven. He is King in that He reigns over His church, indeed over all His creation. We cannot receive Christ as Priest unless He is also our Prophet and King.

It is when we learn by His Word to obey Him that we go forth proclaiming His gospel message to a lost and dying world. And we do not go alone. He is with us always, even to the end of the age.

Be a Soul Winner
The fruit of the righteous is a tree of life,
and he who wins souls is wise (Prov. 11:30).

The tree of life is seen in the garden of Eden (Gen. 2:9; 3:22-24) and in the book of Revelation, (2:7; 22:2, 14, 19) and holds out the promise of eternal life to whoever eats of its fruit. (The phrase is seen only here, and in Proverbs 3:18; 13:12; and 15:4.) Following their eviction from the garden, Adam and Eve looked back and saw cherubim with flaming swords guarding the gates to the garden and the Tree of Life.

In Revelation, quite a different picture is given. Those whose robes are washed are allowed to eat of the fruit of the tree. Oh, the marvelous grace of our God, who turns our sin, rebellion, and consequent death into the joy of eternal life with Him!

As bondslaves of Christ, He calls us to bear the fruit of righteousness that only comes through Him (Phil. 1:11; Gal. 5:22-25). We are, as it were, trees of life planted in this world, and as Christ's ministers of reconciliation (2 Cor. 5:18) are to show forth the fruit of eternal life to all people everywhere.

Scriptural Examples

Jonah. Jonah was called by God to go to Nineveh and be a tree of life. Instead, he rebelled and ran the other way. I'm afraid we are often like Jonah, refusing to hold out the tree of life to a world that is swallowed by sin (Jonah 1:1-3:10).

Paul. Paul won many souls for the Lord. He hoped that his ministry to the Gentiles might cause his own countrymen to respond in repentance and faith (Rom. 11:13-14).

The righteous wife. Peter advised wives how to win their husbands to the Lord: through the purity and reverence of their lives, as they exhibited the fruits of the Spirit (1 Pet. 3:1-2).

The apostles. When told not preach the gospel, Peter exclaimed that they "must obey God rather than men." With joy they held forth the tree of life (Acts 5:16-29; 40-42).

Prayer of Application

Father, thank You for Your gospel of grace. Not through any works of mine am I saved, but only through the life and death of Christ my Savior. He is truly a Tree of Life for me.

Witness with the Kindness of Christ

**21) If your enemy is hungry, give him food to eat;
if he is thirsty, give him water to drink.
22) In doing this, you will heap burning coals on his head,
and the Lord will reward you (Prov. 25:21-22).**

Many years ago, in a far-off land, a man laid down his life for his enemies. Very few of us would dare to even lay down our lives for a friend, yet we are told that while we were His mortal enemies, Christ died for us (Rom. 5:6-8). Almost 2,000 years later this former enemy of Christ felt these "burning coals," and my heart melted in acceptance of the gift which Christ's life, death, and resurrection brought.

You may say, "I've lived a good life, I don't have any enemies." But if your life is "hidden with Christ" (Col. 3:3), you have a world full of enemies. Whoever is an enemy of Christ is also your enemy. Our enemies are right next door, and perhaps within our own homes (Matt. 10:36). It is these people whom Jesus would call us to love, pray for, and treat with the kindness most of us reserve for our closest friends.

Many of us do have enemies, however, and of the type created by our sin, not by our devotion to Christ. It is with these people that this command gets very difficult. We just want to erase their memories from our minds. But I believe that Christ calls us to treat them with an extra special kindness and desire for reconciliation. It is a powerful witness of His saving grace, as the coals that would melt sinful hearts are heaped high. God will reward us greatly (Matt. 5:11-12).

Scriptural Examples

Stephen and Saul. In mortal persecution, something which few of us will be asked to endure, Stephen cried out, "Lord, do not hold this sin against them." Standing nearby was a young man named Saul, who though perhaps not perceiving it then, got a load of burning coals heaped upon his head (Acts 7:59-60).

Prayer of Application

Dear God, give me the courage to be a bold witness of the saving grace of Jesus Christ. Help me to pray for my enemies, and by my kindness to them may they come to know You.

Sow the Seeds of Righteousness
**The lips of the wise spread knowledge;
not so the hearts of fools (Prov. 15:7).**

The wise man first stores up knowledge (Prov. 10:14), then disperses it out of its storehouse. So are we first to get wisdom and understanding (Prov. 4:5) then disperse it to fellow sinners.

The parable of the talents in Matthew 25:14-30 speaks of the principle of sowing seed. The individuals who received five and two talents increased their master's wealth because they sowed that seed money, using it as capital for a business that returned them a profit. In the church, we may apply this principle of seed sowing to utilizing our gifts in the advancement of God's kingdom. We first sow the seeds of the Gospel, expecting a harvest. Then we sow the seeds of God's Word that produce growth in the new Christian. That is the Great Commission (Matt. 28: 19-20)! That is our business!

Notice in the parable that the servant who was given one talent buried it, then accused his master of being a wicked man. His master took the talent from this foolish servant who had not invested wisely, and gave it to one who had been faithful. Lord, help us all to be doers (and distributors) of the Word and not hearers only (James 1:22).

Scriptural Examples
Jesus. Our great Example spread His gospel throughout Israel. Ironically, few seeds sprouted at first, as His own people rejected Him. Later, of course, those seeds would spring up as a great plant filling the earth (Matt. 4:23; 9:35).

Noah. He dispersed the knowledge of God's anger and pending judgment to the pre-Flood generation. He preached for years and had no converts. The hearts of the foolish fail to seek the knowledge of salvation (Gen. 6:22; 2 Peter 2:5).

John the Baptist. This greatest of prophets spread the message of repentance and the coming Kingdom (Luke 3:3).

Prayer of Application
Father, open my lips that I may tell others of Your love. Give me the strength to be a witness for You in the midst of adversity in my family, among my friends, and at my place of work.

Let Living Waters Flow from You

The mouth of the righteous is a fountain of life, but violence overwhelms the mouth of the wicked (Prov. 10:11).

Water is an element that is often used metaphorically in Scripture. For the Jew, the wide and flowing river was a picture of eternality and peace. Ezekiel 47:1-12 speaks of a river issuing forth from the temple of God that becomes so wide and deep that no man can cross it. Trees lined its banks and its waters teemed with fish and swarms of living creatures.

Water also speaks of judgment. Noah and his family rode safely in the ark through the waters of judgment, while everyone else perished (2 Peter 2:5). After the Red Sea opened to allow the Israelites to pass through on its dry bed, the waters raced back in judgment against Pharaoh and all his army (Ex. 14:27-28).

But perhaps water's greatest significance is in its representation of the Holy Spirit. Jesus said in John 7:38-39 that "Whoever believes in me, as the Scripture has said, streams of living water will flow from within him." By this he meant the Holy Spirit. As believers, we are His temple. From us should flow His living water, a fountain of mercy and forgiveness, a flood of graciousness and kindness, a tide of joy and thanksgiving, a river of peace and patience, and a geyser of the gospel of truth. Let His Spirit flow through you and refresh the world.

Scriptural Examples

The woman at the well. This Samaritan woman learned of the living water that Christ gives. Such water would become "a spring of water welling up to eternal life" (John 4:9-14).

The Israelites. God spoke through the prophet Jeremiah about His people who had forsaken Him, the Spring of living water, and had dug their own cisterns that could not hold a drop. They were backslidden and idolatrous, prostituting themselves under every spreading tree (Jer. 2:13-20; 17:13).

Prayer of Application

Lord, thank You for the living waters that flow so freely. May they be in me a spring welling up toward others, inviting them to come – to taste and see that the Lord is good.

Invite Others to the Lamb's Cleansing

**Who can say, "I have kept my heart pure,
I am clean and without sin"? (Prov. 20:9).**

Americans are historically very independent people and want to do things for themselves. But can you imagine do-it-yourself heart surgery?

There you are lying flat on your back on the operating table, looking into a big mirror on the ceiling. Your scalpel is poised on the line drawn on your chest. Beads of perspiration break out on your forehead as you think of the pain that lies ahead, since a general anesthetic would be out of the question. The only sound you hear is that of the steady wheeze of the respirator and your own sickly heart beating uncontrollably.

Sound ridiculous? It is actually not as ridiculous as the heart surgery that millions of people perform on themselves every day. They say, "My heart is clean, I have made it pure." They do not practice surgery, but self-deception. The heart they claim to make pure by good deeds is their eternal soul.

Only one Surgeon can give you a clean heart that is sinless and pure in the sight of God. His name is Jesus, the Lamb of God slain from the foundation of the world. His heart was broken so that many hearts could be eternally healed. Invite others to wash their hearts in His cleansing blood.

Scriptural Examples

David. David was a sinner and acknowledged that fact. Even a great king like David needs cleansing; he cannot do it for himself. In David's wonderful fifty-first Psalm, he asked God to cleanse him from his sin and wash away all his iniquity. He requested a pure heart, freshly created by God, and that all of his past sins would be blotted out of God's record book. Why would a just God do this? For the purpose of His own delight, pleasure, and glory (Ps. 51:1-19).

Prayer of Application

Heavenly Father, thank You for the cleansing blood of Christ by whom every person must be washed if he is to be presentable in Your sight and stand faultless before You.

Get Involved in World Missions
**When the righteous thrive, the people rejoice;
when the wicked rule, the people groan (Prov. 29:2).**

Even though the natural man will badmouth Christianity, he relishes the thought of living in a land where the Word of God reigns over the lives of its citizens. He wants God's benefits, but rejects His requirements. In most countries of the world today, the wicked are ruling and the people are groaning. The suffering of the people gives evidence of the leader's sin.

Political solutions rarely work. Typically they just cause more problems. The only solution is to change people's hearts, because that is where the problem has its root. I know of only one person who can change men's hearts: the Lord Jesus Christ. Only Christ, working through the media of the Holy Spirit, the Word of God, and people like us.

God's "kindness, justice, and righteousness" (Jer. 9:23-24) is to be transported throughout the world (Matt. 28: 19, 20). How? By people like you and me. Now, we can't all go to the foreign field, but we can pray for and financially support those who can go, and who are called to go. Get involved in world missions, to the end that the righteous everywhere will thrive, and the people will rejoice.

Scriptural Examples
The Romans. The ancient Roman world was a paradigm of pagan wickedness and immorality. The rulers were egocentric and corrupt and treated people with cruelty and disinterest. But one day, a small home church was planted in Rome. I suspect Paul had something to do with converting the people who went to Rome, starting this mission by long distance. Within a few centuries, Rome became a thriving center for the Christian faith. Even the government had become ostensibly Christian (Rom. 16).

Prayer of Application
Lord God, You have commanded us to take Your gospel message to a lost and groaning world. Show me where I can help, and let me have a part in bringing rejoicing to the world.

My Personal Action Plan
....

STUDY QUESTIONS

1. Read Isaiah 6. The prophet saw a vison of the perfectly holy God. What was his reaction? Why? What did the seraph do? Why? What did the Lord then say and what was Isaiah's response? What was the Lord's message? How is the Gospel like a message of judgment for some? (Hint: Read 1 Cor. 1:18-25.)

2. In the story of Jonah, what message did God want to send to Nineveh? Why do you suppose Jonah balked at going? (Do you think that there was an ethnic problem?) What happened in Nineveh? Do you think the principal cause of what happened was Jonah? (See 4:2 to see what Jonah thought.) Compare God's feeling about the Ninevites to that of His messenger.

3. In 2 Chronicles 30:1-11 an invitation was given. What was it? Did everyone come? Why not? Did some come? Why?

4. In Athens, Paul preached to the crowds. In Acts 17:32 we are told of their mixed reaction. Is it the same today?

5. In John 6:28-29 Jesus is asked what work must be done to satisfy God's requirements. What is His response? What does the word "believe" mean in this context? Discuss with others.

PROVERBS TO PONDER
9:1-6; 10:20-21; 13:7, 9; 14:5; 16:6

ONE TO MEMORIZE
The fruit of the righteous is a tree of life,
and he who wins souls is wise (Prov. 11:30).

MAKING APPLICATION
My personal action plan to obey the Great Commission:

1)_____ 2)_____

3)_____ 4)_____

·Chapter Seven·
A MAN AND HIS WORLD

Part Three:
Walking In The World

Sometimes, when life closes in around us and the going gets rough, we want to cry out to God, "Beam me up, Lord!" We wonder why God does not take us home to be with Him and let us leave this old world with all its trouble and sin. But He keeps us here. Why? I believe there are two basic reasons.

The first reason we have just reviewed. He wants us to show forth His lovingkindness to this dark and evil world, to the end that He will be glorified on the day of judgment (1 Peter 2:12), and that through our testimony all of His sheep will be gathered into His barn (Ezek. 34:11-16; John 10:14-16).

The second reason is to show to *us* His character and His power to the end that we will find our joy only in Him. Now we see "but a poor reflection as in a mirror" (1 Cor. 13:12), but we do see. Now we "know in part," but we do know. As we "walk" through life on this planet, we are to learn the knowledge of God. In Proverbs 2:1-5, Solomon gives us the reason for studying this book of wisdom. If you search for wisdom, "then you will understand the fear of the Lord and find the knowledge of God." As Paul says in Philippians 3:10, "...that I may know Him...and the fellowship of His sufferings" (KJV).

My prayer is that as you conclude this study, you will just be beginning your search for God's wisdom and will find that He who has begun a good work in you is faithful to complete it (Phil. 1:6).

Make All Your Ways Pleasing to God
A wicked man puts up a bold front
(KJV: "hardeneth his face"), but an upright man gives
thought to his ways (Prov. 21:29).

I once saw a photograph of a man who was running for mayor of a small town. He was in shorts and a T-shirt and punching a body bag. There was a scowl on his face and his T-shirt pictured a skeleton's face with a cigarette dangling out of its mouth. On it were the words, "Who wants to live forever anyway?" It reminded me of the first phrase of this proverb.

The natural man has every reason to suspect that God will one day call him into account (Rom. 1:18-23). But because of the hardness of his heart, unregenerate man puts up a bold front, casting aside the revelation of his Creator in Jesus Christ. He hardens his face in a fearless scowl and chooses to live his life any way he pleases. But as Derek Kidner writes, "A bold front is no substitute for sound principles" (p. 146).

The upright man seeks to live a life of obedience to God. He gives thought to his ways and his entire lifestyle and seeks to please God in all that he thinks, says, and does. The upright man takes the Word of God seriously and applies its truth to all areas of his life, asking the Holy Spirit to assist him in carrying out its demands. Mostly, the upright man lives a life of faith, submitting his body as a living sacrifice to God (Rom. 12:1).

Scriptural Examples

The adulteress. This woman was loud and defiant as she looked for a simpleton to lure into her bed. With a brazen or hardened face she even talked of making offerings to the God she so flagrantly disobeyed (Prov. 7:10-14).

Abraham. What a contrast we see in this upright man. God told him to take Isaac to a mountain and offer him as a burnt sacrifice. Believing God would either stop him or raise Isaac from the dead, Abraham did it (Gen. 22:2-14; Heb. 11:17-19).

Prayer of Application

Dear Lord, thank You for rescuing me from my rebellion, when I, too, set my stony face against Your Word and Your Son. Help me, Lord, to live a life pleasing to You in every way.

Walk in the Strength of the Lord

**29) The way of the Lord is a refuge for the righteous,
but it is the ruin of those who do evil.
30) The righteous will never be uprooted,
but the wicked will not remain in the land (Prov. 10:29-30).**

The KJV renders "refuge" here as "strength," a term Derek Kidner would translate "stronghold." But, of course, the Lord is all of these things. As the psalmist wrote in Psalm 46:1, "God is our refuge *and* strength, a very present help in trouble"(KJV).

What is the *way* of the Lord? It is the path of righteousness upon which each saved person should have his feet firmly planted (Jer. 6:16). But it is an alien way to us, and to attempt to walk it in our own strength is futile. Only God can supply the means to keep His way (2 Sam. 22:33-34).

And how are we to appropriate this strength? It is only through faith in the One who says He will give it to us (Eph. 1:18-20; Phil. 4:13). We need to walk daily by faith, trusting in the One who can deliver us from evil. We need to be rooted and grounded in the Lord Jesus and His Holy Word. But the wicked do not even see their need for strengthening, because there is no inner conflict between evil and righteousness within them.

Scriptural Examples

The Old Testament saints. These people accomplished all sorts of incredible things because "through faith" their "weakness was turned to strength" (Heb. 11:32-34).

Nicodemus. This high-ranking Jewish official timidly came to Jesus to ask about the Kingdom of God (John 3:1-21). Later, we see him strengthened in his faith as he attended to the burial of his Lord by his gifts of myrrh and aloes (John 19:39).

Babylon and Tyre. These ancient cities typify the wicked who think they have strongholds in their earthly wealth and power. It was only a matter of time before they met ruin and destruction (Jer. 51:49-54; Zech. 9:3-4).

Prayer of Application

Sovereign God, Your ways are so much higher than my ways and Your thoughts so far above mine. Teach me Your ways, O Lord, and strengthen me in the path of righteousness.

Live Diligently by Faith

**The way of the sluggard is blocked with thorns,
but the path of the upright is a highway (Prov. 15:19).**

In the Western U.S. there is a hedge called a "natal plum." Its thorns are very sharp. The sluggard, lacking faith, grows in his own mind a barrier out of this kind of hedge that hinders him from seeing life as a highway. At Kadesh Barnea, God sent twelve spies into the Promised Land. Although they liked what they saw, ten of the spies grew such a hedge. The people grew a hedge, too. By their unbelief in the power of God, they refused to go in and take the land. Only Caleb, Joshua, and a few others believed God would give them the victory (Num. 13:30; 14:6, 7).

The faithful man's path is not an easy one, but it is a highway not blocked by a fear that enslaves. Notice that the proverb speaks of the "upright" man and not the "diligent." The upright man follows his Lord's commands. He continues steadfast in prayer, to which he expects an answer. The upright man believes God and acts upon God's Word without delay. To call a man "upright" is to claim diligence for him as well.

Scriptural Examples

Some Thessalonians. Paul said that he heard of some among them who were slothful, disorderly busybodies. He rebuked them for their lack of diligence (2 Thess. 3:10-12).

The slothful and diligent servants. The lazy servant buried his talent, but the faithful servants, entrusted with more, diligently put their master's money to work (Matt. 25:24-30).

The Sodomites. God condemned this wicked city, noted for its evil, arrogance, and apathy (Ezek. 16:48-50).

The young widows. Paul criticized the young widows in the church who were gossips and busy bodies (1 Tim. 5:11-14).

The wife and mother of Proverbs. She was industrious and blessed, overseeing her household with diligence (Prov. 31:27).

Prayer of Application

Dear Lord, keep me on the path of faith. I humbly ask for Your leadership, and the strength to follow You. Let me not build up a hedge of unbelief that blocks the highway before me.

Rest in the Providence of God
Commit to the Lord whatever you do, and your plans will succeed (Prov. 16:3).

Paul enjoins us in Philippians 4:6-7 not to be anxious about anything, but to pray with thanksgiving, that our hearts may be guarded with the peace of God that passes all natural understanding. The key to this peace is absolute trust and confidence in God. Proverbs 3:5-6 reiterates this principle of rest in God.

First, we must understand the God in whom we are called to trust. He is absolutely sovereign and is able to do much more than we give Him credit for. He is subordinate to none. Second, the faith we have in God must be an active faith. It is praying with thanksgiving and believing God hears us, that whatever it is we ask of Him, He can do (Mark 11:24). Finally, it is a faith that steps out with humble trust in the love, power, and provision of God. It is a faith that prays, and then goes to work.

The man who commits the works of his hands, mind, and heart to the glory and honor of the Lord Jesus knows that his steps, plans, and even his every thought will be established and rewarded with eternal treasure in heaven (1 Cor. 3:11-15).

Scriptural Examples

Eliezer. Abraham's servant searched for a bride for Isaac. He committed his way to the Lord and his plans succeeded. He found and brought back Rebekah for his master's son (Gen. 24).

Nehemiah. He prayed that God would help in obtaining approval to rebuild Jerusalem. God established Nehemiah's way and work and the city was restored (Neh. 1:4-11).

Daniel. Daniel purposed in his heart not to defile himself with the king's table, but to follow the ways of the Lord his God. God caused the officials in the king's palace to show favor to Daniel and his friends Shadrach, Meshach, and Abednego. Because of their faith in the God of Israel, their ways were established (Dan. 1:8-9).

Prayer of Application

Provident Lord, help me to trust You fully in all things. I often want to trust in my own resources, and that is idolatry. Cause me to pray fervently and then to work just as fervently.

Make Level Paths for Your Feet

**In the paths of the wicked lie thorns and snares,
but he who guards his soul stays far from them (Prov. 22:5).**

Proverbs 1:17-18 speaks of how the net a wicked man spreads for others only traps himself. But there are other "thorns and snares" that lie in the weeds along the path of the wicked. The following is a short and incomplete list.

There is the trap of disease and sudden death caused by sin. I think of the horrors of AIDS and the terrible effects of crack cocaine. There is the snare of unfulfilled lust from being addicted to pornography. There is the disappointment that comes when sin does not deliver what it promises. There are relational problems like divorce and child abuse. Finally, there is unrelenting guilt and the bondage of the fear of death (Heb. 2:15).

"Well, I'm a Christian," someone says, "and my life hasn't exactly been a bed of roses!" I understand. I, too, have had many troubles as a Christian. But the trials the Christian suffers are purposeful. He is given the sure hope that God's sovereign purposes are being worked out in his life. In "guarding our souls" we avoid the consequences of sinful habits and lifestyles. We have the forgiveness of a loving Father who removes our fear of death. We need to cling to Him by faith and walk on paths made level for our feet (Prov. 4:26; Heb. 12:13).

Scriptural Examples

Job. Job suffered greatly, but his trials give us a behind-the-scenes look into God's providence. Perhaps Job never understood what God's purpose was, but he guarded his soul and was rewarded with doubled prosperity (The Book of Job).

The wicked prophets of Samaria. Jeremiah told of these godless men who followed evil and used their power unjustly. The Lord said that He would make their paths slippery. They would be banished to darkness and disaster (Jer. 23:10-13).

Prayer of Application

Father, keep my feet on level paths that avoid the traps and snares of the unbeliever. Thank You for Your wonderful and loving providence that assures me of a safe journey home.

Do Not Take Your Eyes Off of the Eternal

17) Do not let your heart envy sinners, but always be zealous for the fear of the Lord. 18) There is surely a future hope for you, and your hope will not be cut off (Prov. 23:17-18).

There is an old saying that goes, "He is so heavenly-minded that he is no earthly good." But for every Christian of whom that may be said, there must be ten who are so earthly-minded they are no heavenly good. Why? Because many of us have succumbed to the attractions of this world. We want a temporal reward rather than an eternal one.

Our envy stems from both admiration and resentment. The Christian may feel sorry for himself. He has to play by a different set of rules. He is disciplined by God for something sinners do with applause from others. We are preoccupied with ourselves and with this world. But this world is a will-o'-the-wisp, a fancy that will soon pass away (1 Cor. 7:31).

Jesus commands us to lay up for ourselves eternal treasures in heaven (Matt. 6:19-21). God calls us to a life in this temporal world that is characterized by faith (Rom. 1:17), zealously walking in the fear of the Lord. Sinners work to receive a crown that will not last, but those who are zealous for the fear of the Lord will get a crown that will last forever (1 Cor. 9:25). It is a crown that will be bestowed by the Lord Jesus Himself. But it is a crown that we will have to die to get.

Scriptural Examples

Asaph. In Psalm 73, Asaph tells us of his envy of the wicked. His feet had almost slipped. But he concludes that God is "the strength of my heart and my portion forever."

Elijah. In an amazing story of a man of God who was always zealous in the fear of the Lord, this prophet kept on working for God right up to the time that God took him up to heaven in a whirlwind (2 Kings 2:1-12).

Prayer of Application

Father, thank You for Your eternal hope, a hope that will never be cut off. Help me, Lord, to keep my eyes fixed on Jesus, who assures me that His promise of reward will come to pass.

My Personal Action Plan

STUDY QUESTIONS

1. Read 1 John 1:1-7. Of whom is he speaking in verses 1 and 2? In verse 3, what benefit do we get from John's message? In verse 4, what is John's motivation for writing it to us? In your own words, what is the message of verse 5? Of verse 6?

   Now read 1 John 2:1-6. In verse 2, how are we saved from our sins? In verses 3-5, how do we have assurance that we are saved? Who is our example of how to walk in the world (v.6)?

2. Daniel 3 gives us a story of three men who walked with God. Who were they? What did they refuse to do? What did they say in verses 17 and 18 when the chips were down? In verse 25, a friend of theirs shows up. Who was He? What was the effect of their testimony on the king? What happened then? Does the God of these men still live and work in the world? Are you willing to do as they did?

3. In Joshua 6:1-20, we find others on a "walk" of faith. What happened? Did they conquer in their own strength? Why do you suppose God gave them such a strange battle plan?

PROVERBS TO PONDER
14:26; 15:24; 16:7, 20; 19:2, 23; 20:24

ONE TO MEMORIZE
Trust in the Lord with all your heart and lean not on your own understanding; in all your ways acknowledge him and he will make your pathways straight (Prov. 3:5-6).

MAKING APPLICATION
My personal action plan to walk faithfully with God:

1)_____ 2)_____

3)_____ 4)_____